designer style jewelry

designer
style
jewelry

TECHNIQUES AND PROJECTS FOR ELEGANT DESIGNS FROM CLASSIC TO RETRO

SHERRI HAAB

WATSON-GUPTILL PUBLICATIONS
New York

Copyright © 2004 by Sherri Haab

First published in 2004 by Watson-Guptill Publications,
a division of VNU Business Media, Inc.,
770 Broadway, New York, NY 10003
www.wgpub.com

All projects by Sherri Haab, unless otherwise indicated.
All photography by Dan Haab.

LIBRARY OF CONGRESS CATALOGING-IN-PUBLICATION DATA
Haab, Sherri.
 Designer style jewelry: techniques and projects for elegant designs
from classic to retro / Sherri Haab.
     p. cm.
 Includes index.
 ISBN 0-8230-2601-9 (alk. paper)
 1. Jewelry making. I. Title.

 TT212.H33 2004
 745.594'2--dc22

                              2004010040

Senior Aquisitions Editor: Joy Aquilino
Editor: Michelle Bredeson
Designer: Alexandra Maldonado
Production Manager: Hector Campbell

Manufactured in the U.S.A.

First printing 2004

1 2 3 4 5 6 7 8 9 / 12 11 10 09 08 07 06 05 04

When using cutting tools and other suggested
products, readers are strongly cautioned to follow
manufacturers' directions, to heed warnings, and
to seek prompt medical attention for an injury. In
addition, readers are advised to keep all poten-
tially harmful supplies away from children.

acknowledgments

Thanks to my family: To my husband Dan for the beautiful photographs, to Rachel and Michelle for your creative ideas and photography assistance, and to David for your patience.

To my friends: Thank you for the encouragement, support, and for contributing projects along the way.

Many thanks to the editorial and design staff at Watson Guptill Publications for their dedication to this project.

And thanks to all of the manufacturers who supplied products and technical advice for the projects in this book.

contents

Acknowledgments   5
Introduction   8

getting started   10
Findings   12
Tools   14
Stringing Materials   16
Glues & Adhesives   18

wire jewelry   20
Freshwater Pearl Bracelet   23
   Earrings   *25*
Stone Pendant with
   Wire-Wrapped Bezel   26
Crystal Flower Bracelet   29
   Ring   *33*
Leaves & Violets Bracelet   34
   Earrings   *37*

crocheted jewelry   40
Beaded Gemstone Necklace   43
That '70s Ring   46

shrink Art jewelry   50
Faux Ivory Scrimshaw Pendant   54
   Bracelet   *57*
Vintage Photo Jewelry   58
Celtic Knots Bracelet   61
   Earrings   *65*
   Pendant   *65*
Shrink Hearts   66

polymer clay jewelry 70

Candy-stripe Bangle Bracelets 73

Faux Turquoise Donut Pendant 76
   Bracelet 80

Asian-style Floral Pendant 81
   Pin 85
   Earrings 86

Gold-stamped Kanji Pendant 87

Mica Pearl Pendant 90

resin jewelry 94

Cast Resin Heart Pendant 97

Bottle Cap Pins & Pendants 100

Pressed Flower Pendant
   & Earrings 104
   Bracelet 107

retro picture jewelry 108

Leather Bracelet 111
   Pendant 115
   Barrette 115

Clear Bauble Bracelet 116
   Pendant 119

Vintage Valentine Bracelet 120
   Necklace 123
   Earrings 123

Templates 124

Suppliers 126

Index 128

introduction

I love handmade designer jewelry. I always skip the mass-produced brands and head straight for designer collections found in galleries or high-end stores to see beautiful examples of handmade pieces. The jewelry in these galleries is designed by artists who use many different materials, including wire, glass, resin, fiber, and clay. Each piece has a unique personality because of the craftsmanship of the artist who made it. There are several very well-known artists who make handcrafted pieces that are highly collectable. The handmade pieces I have collected over time increase in meaning and sentimental value as I come to learn more about the artists who designed the pieces and the processes used to create them.

This bracelet and ring set (page 29) is one of a number of projects using wire wrapping techniques.

My earliest memories relating to jewelry go back to when I was just two or three years old, and yes, I really do have memories that young. I was sitting on my grandmother's floor playing with a plastic container filled with beads from a broken necklace. They were white and mocha plastic pearls. A few years later we inherited these beads. I recall using the beads as "pretend pills" and giving one to my "pretend patient," otherwise known as the family cat. The only problem was that the cat wasn't pretending and swallowed the bead. I was horrified and thought I had killed the cat. When I finally worked up enough courage to tell my father, he assured me that the cat wouldn't die, and then patiently waited with me for the cat to "cough up" the bead, for what seemed like an eternity. The beads disappeared after the cat incident and I never saw them again.

I remember making shrink art jewelry before shrink plastic was sold commercially. My mother would buy liver lids from the meat department at the local store. The lids were clear plastic with a red striped pattern around the edge. We would trace comic strip characters with a permanent marker and cut them out to make charm bracelets. If you shrank the whole lid, you would have a really cool pendant with a red striped pattern around the edge. I also made pearl cluster rings with metallic elastic and beads, based on one my made at a women's activity night at church. She taught me how to crochet my own, and I wore it proudly to school. No one remembers the original pattern, but I have recreated it as best as I can remember in this book to make a '70s-style ring. From that point on, I made jewelry out of anything that was accessible to a kid, Play-Doh®, cardboard covered with glitter, beads, telephone wire, aluminum foil, and white glue mixed with food coloring, to name just a few.

Today I still enjoy making jewelry using some of the same materials I used to use back then, along with new products and art supplies. There are a variety of great products you can find in craft stores or through reputable online stores. Beading and jewelrymaking suppliers offer catalogs with a variety of findings and stringing materials to provide the means to finish your creations just like professional jewelry designers.

Leather is easy to work with and can be used to make charming jewelry pieces such as this bracelet (page 111).

I get so excited when I learn a new technique to create a new piece of jewelry. It's really fun to discover that you can make the same kind of jewelry that the designers do with simple, inexpensive craft materials. Making your own jewelry can be very satisfying. It provides a way to express your own personal style and creativity. The projects in this book explore different techniques to help get started making your own collection of handmade designer jewelry.

getting
started

A few simple techniques, findings, and tools are all you need to put together and finish the projects in this book. Once you are familiar with them, it will be easier to concentrate on the creative aspects of designing a piece, and you will have the confidence you need to begin a great project.

findings

Finishing a piece of jewelry is sometimes the most important step in the process of creating it. You want a piece that will hold up and look professional at the same time. The right findings—the metal components that hold a piece of jewelry together—can really enhance a piece. Choose findings that complement the other materials in the piece and don't detract from the overall look you are trying to achieve. Bead shops, craft stores, and catalogs sell a variety of findings for making jewelry. The findings listed here are commonly used in jewelrymaking.

JUMP RINGS are small metal loops that are used to link components together. Jump rings are available in fine or base metal.

SPLIT RINGS are like key rings. You can use them in place of jump rings without having to use pliers. They are great for heavy pieces or stressed areas where you don't want to risk having a jump ring pull apart.

BAILS are decorative loops or connectors that are placed at the top of a pendant and used to hang pendants from chains.

EAR WIRES are available in a variety of styles and metal finishes. Use jump rings or leave holes in your piece to attach purchased ear wires.

HEAD PINS are short wires with a ball or flat pad on one end. You can hang a bead on a head pin and then coil the pin's top to make a loop for hanging.

EYE PINS are similar to head pins, except they have a loop instead of a ball at the bottom. This allows you to hang another piece or bead to dangle from the loop.

PIN BACKS can be glued to the back of a pin with epoxy, or some pin backs come with ready-to-use adhesive strips. They are sold in different sizes and styles. Pin backs are usually available in base metal or sterling silver.

Open jump rings by twisting the ends out to each side with pliers. Close jump rings in the same fashion by bringing the ends back in from the sides.

Don't pull jump rings open and apart. This weakens them by adding stress to the metal.

CLASPS are closures used to join the ends of a necklace or bracelet together. Loop-and-toggle, lobster claw, spring ring, hook-and-eye, and barrel are all types of clasps that are available commercially. Clasps can really add to your overall design, so choose a clasp that complements your piece in style and weight.

CRIMP BEADS are tiny beads used to secure the end of nylon-coated wire. (See page 16 for instructions on using crimp beads.) Crimp beads can also be used to hide knots on the ends of cord for a neat finish. If used on cord, they can simply be glued over the knot or flattened over the knot with a pair of flat-nose pliers.

BEAD TIPS are used to cover knots when stringing with thread. Bead tips have two cups, like a clamshell, that close together to hide the knot and a hook that attaches to a jump ring or clasp. To help secure the knot, apply a drop of glue to it before closing the bead tip.

Findings are the hardware you need to pull your jewelry designs together. Clockwise from top left: Pin backs, loop-and-toggle clasps, lobster claw clasp, ear wires, silver head pins, brass head pins, eye pins, crimp beads, and jump rings.

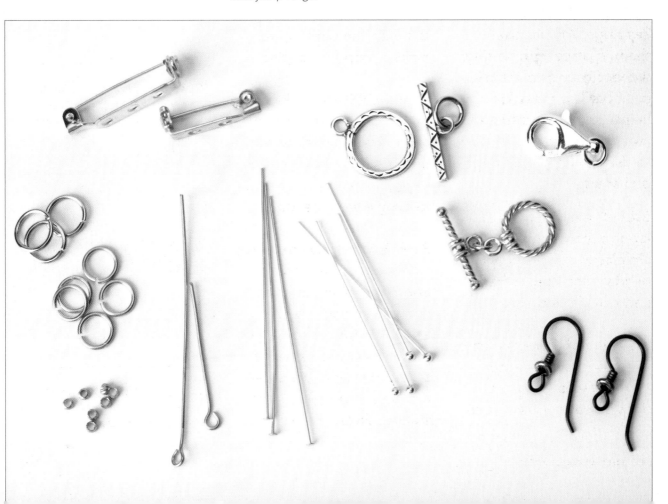

tools

PLIERS

Good quality jeweler's pliers will make a big difference in the quality of your work. There are many types of pliers available. For the projects in this book the basic pliers needed are:

NEEDLE-NOSE PLIERS are common household pliers that have long tapered jaws with teeth.

CHAIN-NOSE PLIERS are used to open and close jump rings. They are also useful for gripping or holding wire or for crimping down the ends of a wire wrap. These are similar to needle-nose pliers, but do not have teeth.

ROUND-NOSE PLIERS are essential for forming wire loops. They have a graduated tip for making loops of various sizes.

FLAT-NOSE PLIERS are useful for holding or gripping wire. You can also use them to bend wire into a 90-degree angle with ease.

You can make all of the projects in this book with a few basic pliers and good-quality wire cutters. Clockwise from top left: crimping pliers, chain-nose pliers, flat-nose pliers, needle-nose pliers, round-nose pliers, and wire cutters.

CRIMPING PLIERS are specialized pliers that are used to pinch the center of crimp beads and secure them to nylon-coated wire (see page 16).

WIRE CUTTERS

A good pair of wire cutters will cut wire cleanly. An old pair of wire cutters or a heavy-duty pair from the hardware store is helpful to have for cutting memory wire or heavy gauge wire, without dulling your good pair of wire cutters.

NEEDLE TOOL

This tool is often used by ceramic or clay artists. You can use it as a scriber or to make holes in clay or other soft materials.

RULER

A ruler with millimeter measurements is helpful when working with beads and wire. You can also use it to measure cord or wire before cutting for a project.

BEAD BOARD

A bead board is a board with channels for laying out beads or other components for necklace design. It has measurements on it and also allows you to check your design before beginning a project.

SCISSORS

Small pointed scissors are great for cutting small pieces of paper, shrink plastic, or laminate. You can get into tight places and make clean cuts with a good pair of stainless steel scissors.

TWEEZERS

Use tweezers to position small beads or rhinestones while gluing them in place. Tweezers are also great for holding beading cord to make tight knots.

COMMON HOUSEHOLD ITEMS

Always keep common household items such as wooden toothpicks, ice cream sticks, and chopsticks on hand for gluing, propping, or positioning tiny elements. You would be surprised how often a toothpick or chopstick turns out to be the perfect tool.

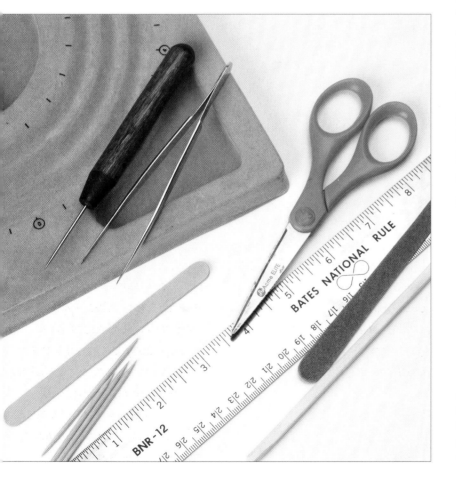

A few helpful items for your toolbox: bead board, needle tool, tweezers, scissors, ruler, nail file, ice cream sticks, toothpicks, and chopsticks.

stringing materials

NYLON-COATED WIRE

Soft Flex® and Beadalon® Tigertail are brand names of beading wire with a nylon coating. Nylon-coated beading wire is available in different gauges and colors. Choose the appropriate gauge for the weight of the bead you are using: thicker gauges for heavier beads and fine gauges for delicate beads. Beading wire is strong and flexible and does not require a beading needle for stringing. It is a good choice for making beaded bracelets as it holds its shape well. Here is how to string and finish a project using coated wire and crimp beads.

1. Slip a crimp bead onto the wire, then string on the clasp. Pull the wire back through the crimp bead and slide the crimp bead close to the clasp.

2. Flatten the bead onto the wires using crimping pliers. There are two channels on the pliers for this crimping process. First crimp the bead in the channel with a dip in the center.

3. Move to the other channel turning the bead sideways to crimp again. The bead will "fold" in on itself for a neat finish.

4. Slide a few beads over the wires to hide the cut end. Continue stringing the rest of the beads. Add a crimp bead and clasp after the last bead. Pull the wire back through the crimp bead and a few of the beads at the end of the strand. Pull until secure. Follow steps 2 and 3 to secure the crimp bead. Use flat-nose or needle-nose pliers to flatten crimp beads for extra security. Clip the excess wire close to the beads.

THREAD

Beading thread is available in synthetic and natural fibers. It can be purchased by the spool or by the card with an attached needle. It comes in a variety of sizes and colors. Some beading threads are made of waxed linen, polyester, or cotton. Jewelry catalogs offer a variety of types to choose from. I prefer silk cord for pearls and delicate beads because it drapes nicely after the beads are strung. Beading thread can be finished by knotting the end and hiding the knot inside a bead tip. Glue the knot before closing the bead tip. You can also hide the knot under a crimp bead, flattening it with flat-nose pliers just enough to secure the bead over the knot. Do not use crimping pliers as you would for nylon-coated beading wire, because the edge of the bead may fray or cut the thread.

Elastic thread and cord are available in bead, craft, or fabric stores. Round elastic comes in colors, clear cord, and metallic gold and silver. Finish the ends of the elastic with a square knot and then apply glue or Fray Check™ for extra security.

LEATHER CORD & CHAIN

Leather cord or artificial sinew is great for larger beads or to complement designs with a natural or ethnic theme. The ends can be wrapped with wire or simply knotted with an accent bead to finish. Round leather cord or flat suede cord is used for some of the projects in this book.

Pendants can also be hung from a chain or a fiber cord such as a rattail or twisted cord.

A bail or large jump ring works well to attach a pendant to a cord or chain.

Leather cord, nylon-coated wire, and silk beading cord are popular stringing materials in jewelry-making. Consider the weight of the beads and the color and style of a project when choosing which material to use.

glues & adhesives

Each type of glue or adhesive has its own properties, making it more suitable for one use than another. Consider the materials you are using and the application process of the adhesive. Something as simple as a fine-tipped applicator can mean the difference between a professional-looking piece and a sticky mess. Read the manufacturer's instructions carefully for proper use and safety precautions. Protect your eyes, skin, and respiratory system. Use proper ventilation and work away from food.

BRAND NAMES

Brand names are mentioned throughout the projects as a guide when looking for supplies, because it can be frustrating trying to figure out which glue to use or what type of wire to buy. You may find other brands that work equally well. There is also a listing of my favorite jewelry suppliers and manufacturers at the end of the book (see page 126). Many of the suppliers are very helpful in choosing the right findings and supplies.

EPOXY RESIN is a two-part mixture that is used on materials with non-porous surfaces, such as rhinestones, metal, or plastic. It can also be used as a clear coating, and color can be added in the form of pigments or dyes. Epoxy is sold under different brand names, such as Devcon 2-Ton®, Devcon 5 Minute® Epoxy, or Envirotex Lite®. (See the chapter "Resin Jewelry" for more information on epoxy resin.)

GEL-TYPE adhesives, such as E6000® and FPC9001™, work well on metal, glass, shrink plastic, and other materials with non-porous surfaces.

SUPER GLUE (cyanoacrylate), such as Krazy Glue or Zap-A-Gap, bonds non-porous surfaces together. The pieces must form a tight contact with no air space—for example, an earring backing glued to a flat surface.

ACRYLIC CEMENT, such as G-S Hypo Cement, dries slowly, which allows you more time to place small parts to non-porous surfaces. This cement has a pinpoint applicator, making is very useful for gluing the end of beading thread or cord to prevent fraying.

When using adhesives in jewelrymaking, choose the best type for the task at hand, whether you're using it to bond metal or plastic, stop cord from fraying, or protect surfaces.

ALL-PURPOSE WHITE GLUE, like Sobo® Craft and Fabric Glue, dries clear and remains flexible. It can be used to seal paper before applying to polymer clay or resin and can be baked with polymer clay.

DECOUPAGE GLUE, such as Mod Podge®, seals paper to protect the surface and is available in a matte or gloss finish. The glue is thin and can be applied with a brush or sponge applicator. Acrylic spray or resin can be used over Mod Podge to prevent a tacky surface.

GEM AND JEWEL GLUES are used to glue gems to porous surfaces like fabric or paper. Gem-Tac™ and Aleene's Jewel-It® are two brand names for this type of glue.

FABRIC HEM SEALANT, such as Fray Check™, dries clear and is used to prevent fraying of cord or beading thread. You can also use it over knots to secure them.

wire
jewelry

Wire is a versatile and practical material for jewelrymaking. It is decorative, as well as functional. You can create elegant pieces using wire wrapping techniques. Use wire to create a sense of repetition for a design or choose the color of the wire to accent the beads or other jewelry elements.

There are many types of wire on the market,

available through jewelry and craft suppliers. Gold, sterling silver, brass, and copper wire are the most common types used for making wire jewelry. Craft stores carry enamel-coated wire in a wide range of wonderful colors. However, because the enamel is baked onto copper, it may be scratched off with a lot of wear. Take this into consideration when choosing wire for your design.

Hard, half-hard, and dead-soft are three degrees of wire hardness. Hard wire is difficult to manipulate for wirework as it is very stiff, but it is often used to make strong components. Half-hard wire is easier to bend and can be formed into loops with pliers. You can make a right angle that will hold its shape with half-hard wire. Dead-soft wire bends and wraps easily with very little resistance. This wire is commonly used in projects involving wrapping. Dead-soft wire can be pulled tightly and evenly as you work.

Wire is available in different shapes and gauges. All of the projects in this book use round wire. The technique or application of the wire will determine the gauge, or thickness, needed for the project. The higher the gauge number, the finer the wire. Heavier 20-gauge wire is good for sturdy wire components. Medium 24-gauge wire is used for making linked loops and dangles with beads. Thinner 26- or 28-gauge wire works well for fine wire wrapping or delicate designs. Be sure to factor in the hardness of the wire as described above when choosing a gauge to use. For example, if you want to use a fine gauge wire that holds its shape, then it may require a higher degree of hardness for a particular project. Conversely, if you want to wrap or manipulate a heavy gauge wire, it may need to be softer.

There are a lot of factors to take into consideration when choosing wire for a project, including gauge, hardness, shape, and color. Craft and hobby stores offer a variety of colorful choices for making inexpensive wire projects.

freshwater pearl
bracelet

Wire wrapping is a fundamental jewelrymaking skill that is used in many projects in this book. Once you get the hang of making loops and wrapping wire, you can use this skill to combine any type of bead with silver, gold, or colored wire. This project combines silver wire and freshwater pearls for a professional-looking bracelet. Vary the design by making wire-wrapped dangles or adding more than one bead to each section of wire.

YOU WILL NEED FOR ONE BRACELET

24-gauge, half-hard sterling silver wire

Wire cutters

Ten to fifteen medium- to large-size pearls

Chain-nose or flat-nose pliers

Round-nose pliers

Loop-and-toggle clasp

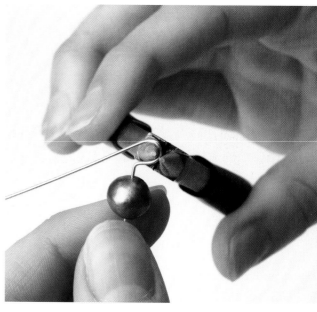

1. Cut off a 12-inch length of wire (cut new pieces as you need them). You can string one pearl on the wire now or wait until step 3. Bend the wire toward you at a 90-degree angle with the chain-nose or flat-nose pliers.

2. Switch to the round-nose pliers and wrap the wire around the pliers away from you to form a loop.

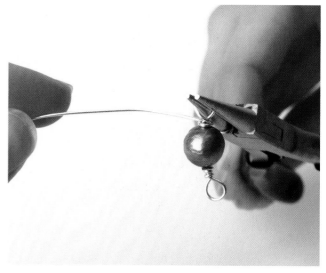

3. Wrap the wire around the base of the loop several times to secure. Add the pearl now if you didn't do so in step 1.

4. Repeat steps 1 through 3 to make a wrapped loop at the other end of the pearl, wrapping close to the pearl. Clip off the excess wire on both ends. Use the tip of the chain-nose pliers to pinch the end of the wire down to prevent it from snagging.

5. Continue making wire loops with pearls, linking them together *before* you wrap. Check the bracelet against your wrist for size as you work. Add a loop-and-toggle clasp by wire wrapping a loop finding on one end of the bracelet and a toggle on the other.

PEARL EARRINGS

To make a pair of wire and pearl earrings, you will need silver wire, two pearls, two small beads, two head pins, and two ear wires. Follow steps 1 through 4 of the bracelet instructions to wrap two pearls with loops at either end. Add a bead to each head pin and link head pins to pearls with wrapped loops. Open the loops on the ear wires to attach the pearls.

stone pendant
with wire-wrapped bezel

Making a wire bezel is a great way to set off a large stone bead. Intricate wire-wrapped designs like this one are appearing in exclusive designer collections as a favorite for gemstone bead designs. You can make your own version easily for a fraction of the cost.

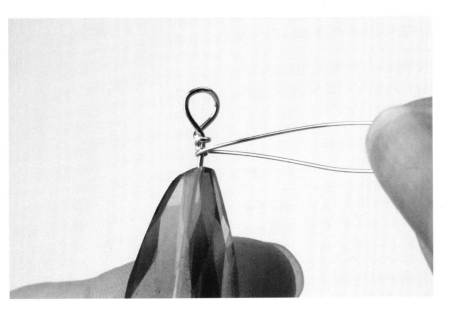

YOU WILL NEED FOR ONE PENDANT

24-gauge, half-hard sterling silver wire

Wire cutters

Chain-nose (or flat-nose) and round-nose pliers

26-gauge, dead-soft sterling silver or fine silver wire

Large, faceted semiprecious stone

Six smaller stones

1. Cut a 12-inch piece of the 24-gauge wire and string the large stone onto it. Wrap a loop at the top and bottom of the stone (see steps 1 through 4 of the pearl bracelet instructions on page 24). Wrap just once around, without wrapping too tightly next to the stone. You want to leave a little "slack" to add the wrapped bezel wire.

2. Measure off about 24 to 30 inches of the 26-gauge wire. Leave about 8 to 10 inches for a "core" wire and the rest of the wire for a "wrapping" wire. Wrap the "core" wire a few times just under the wrapped loop at the top of the stone.

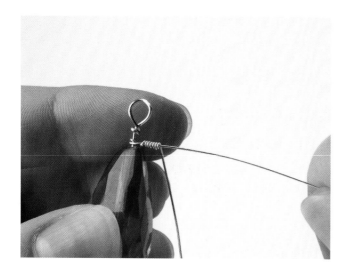

3. Holding the core wire firmly, begin wrapping the wrapping wire around the core wire. Wrap tightly and evenly as you go. Keep wrapping until you come to the bottom of the stone. Wrap the core wire a few times around the base of the wire loop at the bottom of the stone.

4. Rotate the stone as you wrap and continue wrapping around the other side of the stone until you have completed the circumference of the stone. (In this photo, the stone is shown turned upside down.)

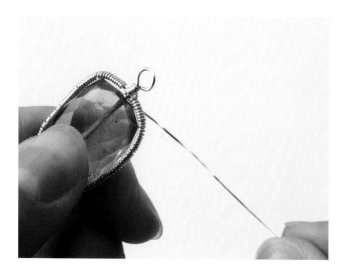

5. When you reach the top of the bead, wrap the core wire around the base of the wire loop a few times to secure. Clip off both wires to finish. Hang the pendant from a sterling silver chain or add accent beads (see instructions at right).

ADDING ACCENT BEADS

To add accent beads to the pendant, use 24-gauge wire to make a wrapped loop linked to the large central stone. Add three beads and finish with a loop linking to a silver chain. Wrap about three times around and clip to finish. Add three beads to the other side in the same manner. You can also add a bead dangle to the bottom of the pendant by stringing a small bead onto a head pin and connecting the head pin to the large central stone with a wrapped loop.

crystal flower
bracelet

Floral designs made with wire and beads are perfect for making jewelry for special occasions. Use clear crystals and white pearls to make breathtaking designs for a bridal party. Brightly colored beads and wire are perfect to accessorize a party or prom dress. You can also pick up the colors from your favorite casual outfit to make a piece to wear every day.

YOU WILL NEED FOR ONE BRACELET

28-gauge, red-colored wire (Artistic Wire™)

Wire cutters

Gold spring ring or lobster claw clasp

Forty 11/0 or 10/0 clear light green seed beads

Four 5mm olive crystal beads (diamond-shaped)

Forty 3mm red crystal beads (fire-polished, AB finish)

Five 5mm fuchsia crystal beads (diamond-shaped)

BEADING BASICS

Beads are a jewelrymaking staple. They can be woven or strung on beading cord or nylon-coated wire, and make great embellishments when sewn or glued onto other pieces. Beads come in such a variety of shapes, sizes, and materials that it's helpful to be familiar with some basic beading terms when choosing beads for a project.

You can find handmade and mass-produced beads made from glass, crystal, semiprecious gemstones (such as amethyst and garnet), shell, pearl, clay, bone, metal, plastic, or wood. Seed beads are tiny glass beads that have been heated and formed into rounded oval shapes. They come in hundreds of colors and finishes as well as different sizes and can be smooth or faceted.

Most beads are measured in millimeters, but seeds beads are measured in "aughts," which are indicated as 11/o, 8/o, etc. The larger the number the smaller the bead.

Charlottes, also called true- or one-cuts, are seed beads with one facet. An "E" bead, or pony bead, is a large (size 5/o or 6/o) seed bead. Some other types of beads include fire-polished beads, which are crystal beads from the Czech Republic that have been shaped in a mold and then flame-polished for a smooth shiny finish, and lamp-worked beads, which are made from glass that has been melted and then molded around a wire.

Beads are available in various finishes, often in combination. Translucent beads let some light pass through. Opaque beads allow no light to pass through. Matte (and semi-matte) beads have the least reflective finish. Iris and Aurora Borealis (AB) finishes are iridescent, multicolored coatings that make the beads shimmer.

With so many choices, you should have no trouble finding the perfect beads for your jewelry designs.

1. Cut a 54-inch piece of wire. Bend the wire in half and slide the clasp to the middle of the wire. Loop one end of the wire through the clasp (go around twice for extra strength). You will now have two strands of wire attached to the clasp. Twist the two strands six to eight times or for about 1/2 inch.

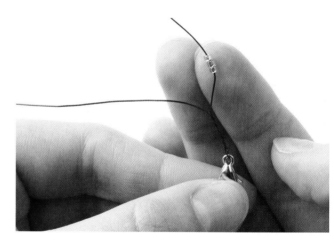

2. Pull one of the wires out to the side and add three green seed beads about 1/4 inch away from where the two strands split.
HINT: As you pull the wire through the beads with one hand, use your other hand to keep the wire from getting caught or kinking, which could cause it to break. Never pull the wire too tight or force it through the beads. If the wire breaks, you can work a new piece into the design by twisting the ends of the new wire and the broken wire. Hide the ends as you work.

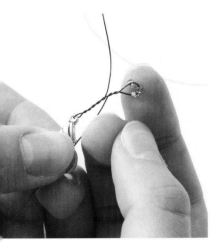

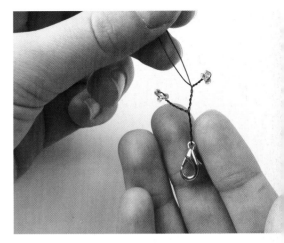

3. Make a loop with the seed beads and twist back down to meet the other strand.

4. Twist the two strands again about five times or for $1/4$ inch.

5. (One strand will now be longer than the other; alternate wires as you add beads to each side to keep the strands relatively equal in length. Add three green seed beads to the opposite side and twist as explained in step 3. Repeat step 4. Add a third set of beads, repeating steps 3 and 4 again.

6. Repeat steps 2 through 4, substituting one olive crystal bead for the three seed beads.

7. To make a red flower, add eight red crystal beads onto one of the wires. Form a circle of beads by threading the wire back through the first bead.

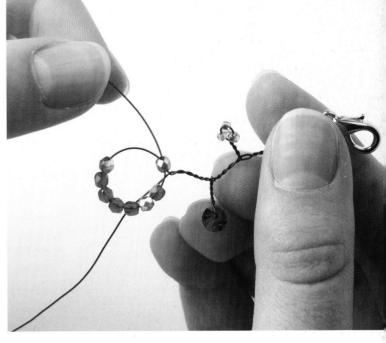

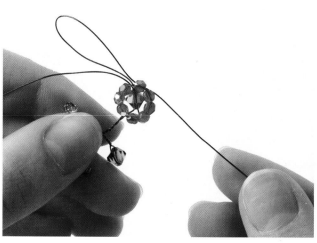

8. Slide a fuchsia crystal bead onto both wires so that it hangs in the center of the circle of red beads.

9. Pull the wires tightly. Thread the wire that was used to form the circle back through the fourth bead in the circle. Continue twisting both wires down the center about six times or for about $1/4$ inch.

10. Continue the pattern as shown. Measure the bracelet to your wrist as you work.

11. Finish the bracelet by twisting the wires for about 1 inch. Make a loop and twist the ends at the base of the loop several times to secure. Clip off the ends of the wires.

FLOWER RING

To make a ring, follow steps 7 through 9 of the instructions for the bracelet to make a flower, but don't twist the two strands together. After forming the flower, add two green seed beads to one of the wires. Thread the other wire through the seed beads in the opposite direction, pulling tightly. Continue adding rows of two beads each until the ring fits your finger. Finish by threading the wires back through the other side of the flower to connect. Clip and tuck the excess wire into a bead to hide.

leaves & violets
bracelet

Gemstones, pearls, and glass beads combine to create a delicate floral vine design. Feel free to personalize the design by using other types of beads or changing the color of the wire. For a funky, casual style, make the bracelet using bright glass, resin, or plastic beads and colorful wire. You can also make a matching choker using the same techniques.

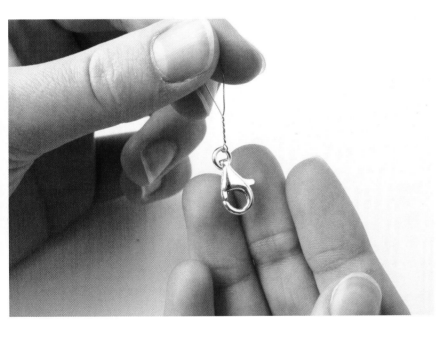

YOU WILL NEED FOR ONE BRACELET

28-gauge, silver-colored wire (Artistic Wire)

Wire cutters

Silver lobster claw clasp

Five leaf-shaped clear green glass beads (Blue Moon Beads)

Eighteen 3mm round faceted purple crystal beads (fire-polished, AB finish)

Five 4mm round olive-green crystal beads

Five 4mm pear-shaped garnets

Five 5mm round light gray or cream-colored pearls

Eighteen 3mm round faceted light amethyst crystal beads (fire-polished, AB finish)

1. Cut a piece of wire 54 inches long. Bend the wire in half and slide the clasp to the middle of the wire. Loop one of the ends of the wire through the clasp (go around twice for extra strength). You will now have two strands of wire attached to the clasp. Twist the strands of wire together about five times to get started, or until you have a little more than ¼ inch.

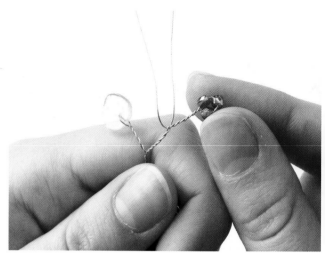

2. Pull one of the wires out to the side. Thread a leaf bead onto the wire, about $1/4$ inch from the end of the twist. Twist the wire back down from the leaf bead until it meets where you left off in the center in step 1.

3. Continue to twist both strands down the center about four or five times or about $1/4$ inch. (One strand will now be longer than the other; alternate wires as you add beads to each side to keep the strands relatively even in length.) Pull the longer strand out to the side, and add three purple beads about $1/4$ inch from the twist. Make a loop with the three beads and twist back down to meet the center. Twist both wire strands together again down the center for another four or five times or about $1/4$ inch.

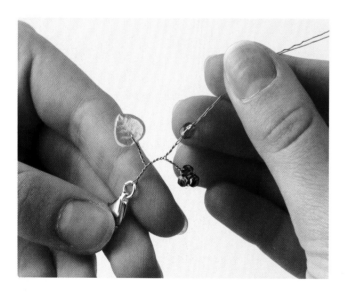

4. Slide an olive-green bead over the twisted wires in the center.

5. Using the opposite wire from the one you strung the purple beads on, add a garnet about $1/4$ inch from the center. Twist back to the center.

6. Add a pearl next and then a group of three amethyst beads, twisting between each addition. Continue adding beads, following the progression shown. Measure the bracelet against your wrist as you go to check the length. Add more beads to the pattern if needed, or add space by adding twists to the center wire between each bead. Finish off by twisting the wires for about 1 inch. Make a small loop with the twist and wrap the ends around several times to secure. Clip the ends off.

LEAVES & VIOLETS EARRINGS

You can easily make a pair of matching earrings using the same techniques as for the bracelet. You need only a few beads, a little bit of wire, and two ear wires.

YOU WILL NEED FOR ONE PAIR OF EARRINGS

28-gauge, silver-colored wire (Artistic Wire)

Wire cutters

Two silver ear wires

Four leaf-shaped clear green glass beads (Blue Moon Beads)

Six 3mm light amethyst round faceted crystal beads (fire-polished, AB finish)

Six 3mm round faceted purple crystal beads (fire-polished, AB finish)

Two 4mm pear-shaped garnets

Two 4mm round olive-green crystal beads

Two 5mm round light gray or cream-colored pearls

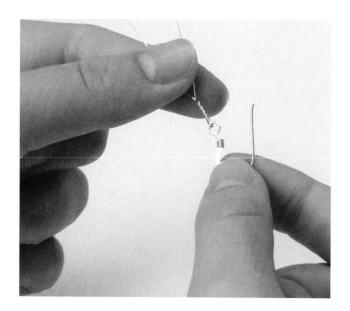

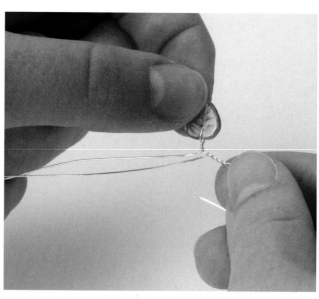

1. Cut a piece of wire 12 inches long. Bend the wire in half and thread it through the ear wire. Twist the wire about three times to secure.

2. Pull one of the strands out to the side. Thread a leaf bead onto the wire, about $1/8$ to $1/4$ inch from the end of the twist. Twist back to the center.

3. Add three amethyst beads to the other wire about $1/4$ inch away from the center twist. Twist back to the center. Twist the two wire strands in the center for about four twists or $1/4$ inch.

4. Add three purple beads and another leaf bead as directed in steps 2 and 3, placing them on opposite sides. Twist the wires in the center for about four twists or $1/4$ inch.

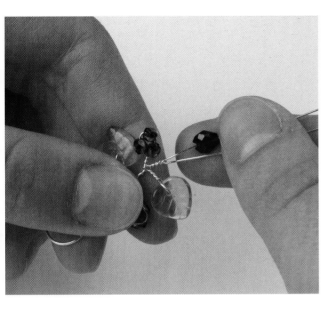

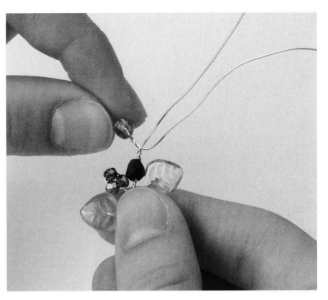

5. Slide a garnet bead over one of the wires in the center. Twist the center wires together a couple of times.

6. Pull one of the wires out to the side. Add one olive-green bead very close to the center. Twist back down to the center wires.

7. Slide a pearl onto the other wire about ¹/4 inch from the wire with the olive bead. Twist back to the center and clip the wire. Twist the existing wire (from the olive bead) into the center twist. Clip off the end.

crocheted
jewelry

Crocheted jewelry has become increasingly popular in designer jewelry collections. Brightly colored fibers and stones provide a variety of exciting possibilities for contemporary designs. Crocheted jewelry can be worn with casual or formal attire, and it has a wide appeal for all ages.

Crocheting isn't just for making sweaters

and afghans. Looking back through history you will find examples of tatting, crocheting, knitting, and macramé used for personal adornment and functional items. Pioneers wove jewelry using hair, silk, or whatever they had available to make intricate designs that were passed down through generations. Today's jewelry designers make crocheted pieces ranging from antique Victorian to bold macramé styles inspired by the 1970s.

All of the crocheted jewelry in this book is created using a simple chain stitch. The materials needed to make a necklace are affordable and easy to obtain. One practical bonus of fiber jewelry is that it is a great alternative for someone who is allergic to metal. Most of all, needlework is relaxing and enjoyable. It is very satisfying to make an heirloom piece that you can wear yourself or give as a lovely handmade gift.

Basic crocheting supplies are inexpensive and readily available. Once you master a couple of basic stitches you can experiment with different beads and beading cord to create an endless number of jewelry designs.

Bead shops carry a variety of stringing materials, both synthetic and natural. Silk beading cord seems to look more elegant than nylon cord for a finished necklace. Silk cord is easy to crochet with and drapes nicely. Before beginning to crochet, unwind the cord from the card and dampen it. This will help straighten out the cord.

Experiment with different weights of cord and sizes of beads. Adjust the size of the crochet hook to the weight of the cord and also to the size of the stitch. You can crochet with many different threads and fibers, including elastic thread, which is used for the '70s-style ring in this chapter. If you have experience with crocheting, experiment with different stitches to create more elaborate patterns.

beaded gemstone
necklace

The necklaces in this project were crocheted using a simple chain stitch with silk beading cord. The cord is very light and comfortable to wear, making it perfect for all kinds of jewelry. Try making an anklet or bracelet using the same techniques and materials. Wear multiple strands or try different crochet stitches to create a variety of styles. The possibilities are endless!

YOU WILL NEED FOR ONE VIOLET PEARL NECKLACE

2-meter card of size 2 silk beading cord (Griffin)

Small steel crochet hook (size 8 to 10)

Size 11/o seed beads (one small package or one strand from a hank)

Thirty-two freshwater pearls

Thirty-four small faceted semi-precious light amethyst gemstones

Two crimp beads

Loop-and-toggle clasp

Acrylic cement or Fray Check

Larger bead or pearl

Head pin

Chain-nose (or flat-nose) pliers

Round-nose pliers

Wire cutters

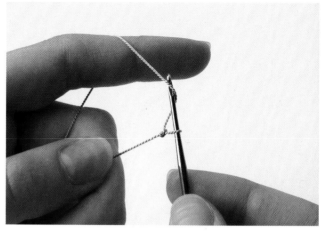

1. Unwind the beading cord from the card. Start with a slip knot at the end of the cord (not the end with the bead needle). To make a slip knot, wind the yarn over itself to make a loop. With the crochet hook, Pull a second loop of cord up through this loop and pull to tighten around the crochet hook.

2. Holding the hook in one hand and the cord in the other, wrap the long end of the cord around the hook. Catch the cord with the hook and pull the cord through the slip knot. The cord you just pulled through will now be on the hook. Do the same thing again and you will have made two chain stitches.

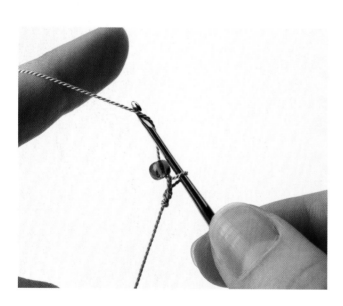

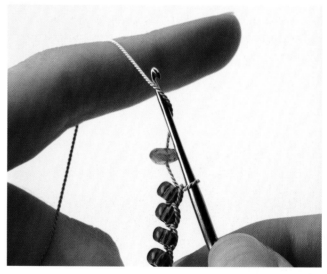

3. Slide a seed bead onto the cord and make one chain stitch. Repeat this step for about thirty seed beads.

4. From this point you can follow various patterns and use different seed beads, pearls, and gemstones to create different looks. To make the the violet pearl necklace on page 43, continue chaining beads as in step 3 with the following sequence, chaining between each bead: Add one amethyst, three seed beads, one pearl, three seed beads, one amethyst, and three seed beads.

5. Add three pearls all at once, followed by one chain stitch. This will make a cluster. Do not pull the cord too tight. Chain three seed beads as in step 3. Add three amethyst beads followed by one chain stitch to make another cluster. Chain three seed beads as in step 3. Continue this sequence until you have ten clusters (five pearl clusters and five amethyst clusters). After the tenth cluster, chain six seed beads. This will be the center of the necklace. Continue up the other side of the necklace, following the pattern in reverse to match the first side.

6. Slide a crimp bead onto the end of the cord and then thread the cord through the loop-and-toggle clasp. Run the cord back through the crimp bead. Knot the cord under the crimp bead. Clip the cord and add a dab of glue.

7. Use chain-nose or flat-nose pliers to flatten the bead over the knot. Repeat steps 6 and 7 on the other end of the necklace.

8. To make a dangle for the center of the necklace, slide a large bead or beads onto a head pin. Make a loop to hang over seed beads in the center of the necklace. Wrap the wire around a few times and clip to finish the dangle (see steps 1 through 3 on page 24 for instructions on making wrapped wire loops).

crocheted jewelry

that '70s ring

Everything old is new again, and retro styles from the 1960s and '70s have made a big fashion comeback. Retro style brings back geometric shapes, big beads, and colorful plastic. It's the type of jewelry that you can wear just for fun. Beaded rings are a blast from the past that you can make to match a groovy retro outfit.

YOU WILL NEED FOR ONE RING

Two yards metallic elastic thread

Small steel crochet hook (size 6)

Fifteen 3-, 4-, or 5mm plastic faceted or pearl beads (with holes large enough for elastic to pass through)

1. Leaving a 24-inch tail of elastic, make a slip knot on the crochet hook (see step 1 on page 44). Holding the hook in one hand and the elastic thread in the other, wrap the long end of the thread around the hook.

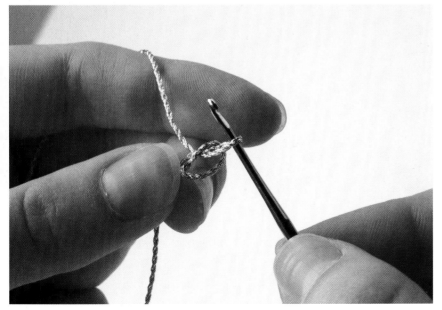

2. Catch the thread with the hook and pull the thread through the slip knot. The thread you just pulled through will now be on the hook. You have made one chain stitch.

3. Make four more chain stitches in the same way for a total of five stitches.

4. Insert the hook into the first chain stitch to form a ring. Wrap the elastic thread around the hook as for a chain stitch, then pull the elastic through both loops on the hook. This is called a slip stitch. You now have a loop on your hook.

5. String a bead onto the elastic. Insert the hook into the next chain stitch in the ring and grab the elastic thread with the hook.

6. Pull the elastic thread through both loops on the hook (slip stitch).

7. Add four more beads to the elastic, slip stitching after each bead around the ring. You will have a total of five beads crocheted around the ring.

8. The next round is worked without beads. Slip stitch twice in each stitch from the previous round (ten slip stitches).

9. Add ten beads, slip stitching one bead onto each of the stitches from the previous round (just as you did in step 6).

10. Slip hook up through the center of the bead cluster and grab the tail to bring it to the wrong side (stretching the elastic will help you to bring the tail through without catching the hook).

11. Crochet a chain stitch with both strands (tail and working elastic) until the chain fits your finger (at least twenty to twenty-five stitches). Finish by hooking through to the opposite side of the bead cluster with a slip stitch. Pull the ends of the elastic all the way through the loop, pulling tightly to fasten off. Weave the ends through a few stitches to hide, and clip off excess.

VARIATIONS

You can make several different crocheted rings, simply by varying the number, placement, and size of beads. For a single bead design, chain stitch a double strand of elastic thread long enough to fit halfway around your finger. Slide the bead down both strands and continue to chain until the ring fits your finger. If you want beads around the entire ring, use small beads and chain one stitch without a bead in between each beaded stitch. Another possible design is to have one large central bead with one smaller bead on each side.

crocheted jewelry

shrink art
jewelry

Jewelry artists have discovered new and innovative techniques to incorporate shrink plastic into their designs. It can be colored with pencils, acrylic paint, or chalk to create elegant pendants, pins, bracelets, and more in myriad colors and effects. Shrink plastic is not just for kids anymore!

Shrink plastic has been available in sheet

form since the early 1970s. It was first introduced on the market under the brand name Shrinky Dinks®. Other brands are now available.

Shrink plastic is sold in transparent, frosted, ivory, brown, and black sheets. There are even new types of shrink plastic that can be used with an ink jet printer. When heated, shrink plastic shrinks to about half of its original size and becomes a thick rigid piece of plastic about 1/16-inch thick.

Shrink plastic holds color better if it is sanded first. Use 320- or 400-grit wet/dry sandpaper and rinse the paper in water as you sand to prevent the plastic dust from building up. Sand horizontally and vertically over the entire sheet. Sanding the back side will help pieces adhere when gluing them together. Shrinky Dinks sells a product called Ruff N' Ready that is presanded. Ruff N' Ready is a convenient, ready-to-use sheet of plastic that holds color very well. Leaving shrink plastic unsanded results in a smooth shiny glass-like surface. It is best to use unsanded shrink plastic if you want the plastic to be clear and shiny after shrinking. Use permanent markers or stamped images to add details to the surface of smooth plastic.

To add solid color to shrink plastic, use colored pencils or acrylic paints. Prisma® and Crayola® brand colored pencils work very well on shrink plastic. You can use acrylic paints and fabric paints, applying the paint in thin layers to the plastic (the colors intensify as the plastic shrinks). Colored chalks can be rubbed over the plastic to create bright or subtle colors depending on how much you apply. Permanent markers and some rubber stamp inks are also great choices for use on the plastic.

After you have created a design, cut out the plastic with small pointed scissors. Holes can be punched at this stage, which is easier than drilling holes after the plastic is heated. Make sure the holes are punched in far enough not to tear and remember that the holes shrink too. A 3/16- or 1/4-inch hole punch will give you a nice small hole for adding jump rings after shrinking.

To bake shrink plastic you can use a regular conventional oven or a handheld heat gun. To shrink in the oven, place the pieces on a glass baking sheet or on a clean sheet of regular white paper. Preheat the oven to 275°F to 325°F. Some brands and types of plastic differ in baking temperature; refer to manufacturer's guidelines for baking temperatures for the type of plastic you are using. The plastic pieces usually take only a few minutes to shrink. The plastic will curl up while heating and then flatten back down after shrinking. If a piece sticks to itself, remove it from the oven and quickly try to pull it apart using oven mitts or hot pads to avoid burning your fingers. Return the piece to the oven and reheat it. It's a good idea to try a few sample pieces before you heat and shrink your project.

Heat guns designed for rubber stamping allow you to heat one piece at a time. This is particularly helpful if you want to make an intaglio (raised) relief pattern on the plastic. You can do this by stamping the plastic immediately after it shrinks with a patterned rubber stamp. Work on a cookie sheet on a heatproof surface. Heat guns get very hot. Wooden chopsticks are handy for holding the plastic in place while shrinking, as heat guns tend to blow the plastic around.

If you are not making a relief pattern on the plastic, immediately after pieces have been shrunk, flatten them by pressing a tile or acrylic block over the plastic. You can also bend or shape the hot plastic over a curved or domed surface.

You can produce an amazing variety of shrink art pieces using different colors and textures of shrink plastic, acrylic paints, and rubber stamps.

Finish your pieces by lightly sanding the corners or edges if needed. Protect the surface of your finished piece by sealing the plastic with a protective coating. Acrylic spray sealants, such as Krylon Crystal Clear, will seal the surface of rubber stamp ink, ink jet ink or other water soluble mediums after baking. You can also use epoxy resin to coat the surface for a high gloss finish. Solvent-based inks and permanent pens should be sealed with a coating of water-based varnish or lacquer, such as 3-D Crystal Lacquer (acrylic sprays will react with permanent inks, causing them to bleed).

You can also glue finished pieces together. Shrinky Dinks® brand recommends using E6000 glue. Sand the pieces to roughen the surfaces before gluing.

faux ivory scrimshaw
pendant

Scrimshaw is the art of engraving or carving images onto ivory or bone and then applying India ink to the carving. New England whalers in the 1800s developed and refined this art with intricate pieces depicting nautical and wildlife themes. Artists who practice the art of scrimshaw today use imitative ivory because of the ban on and protection of ivory. This project uses almond-colored shrink plastic and rubber stamps with images of wildlife to make jewelry reminiscent of traditional folk art scrimshaw.

1. Scratch the plastic with sandpaper in one direction only. Go over the plastic sparingly; scratch the same area only once.

YOU WILL NEED FOR ONE NECKLACE

Almond-colored shrink plastic (Shrinky Dinks)

400-grit sandpaper

Medium brown decorating chalk (National Artcraft Co.)

Rubber stamps

Brown ink pad (StazOn™ by Tsukineko®)

Scissors

3/16- or 1/4-inch round hole punch

Embossing heat tool (or use oven to heat)

Acrylic block

Two large jump rings

Beads and head pins for dangles

24-inch velvet suede lace (The Leather Factory®)

Small jump ring

Lobster claw clasp

26- or 28-gauge brass or copper wire

Wire cutters

2. Rub chalk over the surface lightly. This will bring out the scratches to make an ivory grain pattern.

3. Press the rubber stamp into the ink pad and stamp the image onto the plastic.

4. Trace and cut around the stamped image (see templates on page 125). Be careful not to smear the ink at this stage. Punch a hole at the top for hanging. You can also punch holes at the bottom for dangles if you wish.

5. Heat and shrink the shapes.

6. Use an acrylic block to flatten the shape if needed.

7. Attach a large jump ring at the top of the piece. Add bead dangles using head pins if desired (see steps 1 through 3 on page 24 for instructions on making wrapped wire loops). Thread the pendant onto suede lace, measuring the suede to a desired length. Attach a large jump ring to one side and a small jump ring with a lobster claw clasp to the other side. Wrap brass or copper wire to secure the ends of the suede lace (see steps 7 through 12 on pages 113 and 114 for instructions on wrapping cord with wire). Clip the excess suede to finish.

If you want a nice curved shape to the piece, you can quickly place the hot plastic over a ceramic mug at the end of the heating process. Apply a little pressure using an acrylic block to press the plastic around the curve of the mug.

FAUX IVORY BRACELET

To make a bracelet, follow steps 1 through 4 for the necklace, cutting out a narrow rectangle and punching two holes on each end of the rectangle. Shrink and finish the piece as directed for the necklace.

Attach a 12-inch piece of leather cord to the finished shape using a lark's head knot. For this example I used a 2mm natural-colored round leather lace (The Leather Factory). To make a knot, fold the cord in half to form a loop. Thread the ends of the cord through the holes on one side of the shape and bring both through the loop. Finish the bracelet by adding a lobster claw clasp as directed for the pendant in step 7.

vintage photo
jewelry

You can transfer photos right onto shrink plastic using your ink jet printer. For this project, black and ivory-colored shrink plastic complement sepia-toned photographs to make Victorian-style pendants and earrings. Jewelry sets inspired by themes such as holiday celebrations, weddings, and baby or pet photos make great gifts. Use color photos with brightly colored wire and beads for a whimsical look.

YOU WILL NEED FOR ONE PENDANT OR PAIR OF EARRINGS

Old family photos

Shrinky Dinks plastic for ink jet printers

Scissors

Almond-colored or black shrink plastic (Shrinky Dinks)

3/16- or 1/4-inch hole punch

400-grit sandpaper or nail file

Acrylic spray sealer

Epoxy resin (optional)

Gold or silver leafing pen

E6000 glue or FPC 9001 adhesive

1. Scan family photos and prepare in the computer using a photo editing program. Size images to twice the desired finished size and lighten to 50-percent opacity. The images will look faded or washed out, but will intensify when shrunk. Print the images on the shrink plastic following the package instructions carefully. Trace the images using templates (see page 125) or a ruler, and cut out.

2. Cut out larger background shapes in almond-colored or black shrink plastic. Punch a hole at the top, and one at the bottom if you wish to add a dangle. Shrink the images and background pieces in the oven at 300°F following manufacturer's instructions. Sand the edges lightly to shape. Coat the surface with acrylic spray to protect and seal the images, following with epoxy resin if you want a shiny surface.

3. Add gold or silver around the edges of the pieces with a leafing pen.

FINISHING THE NECKLACE AND EARRINGS

To make a necklace, use wire-wrapped loops (see steps 1 through 3 on page 24 for instructions on making wrapped wire loops) to link faceted crystal beads. Attach the pendant to the necklace using a wrapped wire loop. You can add dangles to the bottom of the pendant with beads and head pins. Add a clasp to finish.

To make earrings, flip the image in the computer to print mirror images. Attach ear wires and beads with wrapped wire loops to complete.

4. Glue the image pieces to the background pieces.

celtic knots
bracelet

One surprising feature of shrink plastic is its usefulness in producing imitative effects. Sea glass, metal, wood, and ivory are a few faux effects that can be achieved using various methods and materials on the surface of the plastic. With black shrink plastic and metallic paste you can make comfortable, light-weight jewelry that has the feel of ancient forged bronze.

YOU WILL NEED FOR ONE BRACELET

Black shrink plastic (Shrinky Dinks)

400-grit sandpaper

Fine permanent marker or light-colored pencil

Scissors

3/16- or 1/4-inch round hole punch

Embossing heat tool

Celtic Knots rubber stamp set (Aspen Art Stamps)

Celtic Wishes rubber stamp set (Aspen Art Stamps)

Rub-On Metallic Highlights paste in copper (Bright Colors set; National Artcraft Co.)

Acrylic spray sealer

Copper- or rust-colored permanent metallic rubber stamp ink pad

3-foot-long piece of 24-gauge copper wire

Chain-nose (or flat-nose) pliers

Round-nose pliers

Wire cutters

Lobster claw clasp

Large jump ring

Small jump ring

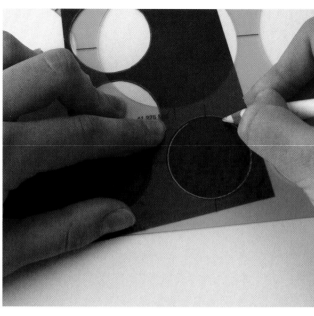

1. Sand the shrink plastic both vertically and horizontally to create a matte surface.

2. Trace shapes with marker or pencil and cut out with scissors (see templates on page 124).

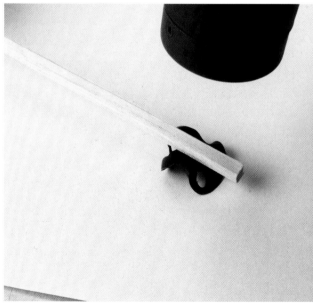

3. Punch holes on each side of each shape.

4. Heat the shapes one at a time with the embossing heat tool.

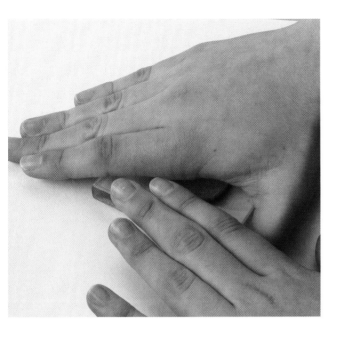

5. As soon as the shapes are completely shrunk, press a rubber stamp firmly on the hot plastic. Press hard, shifting your weight over your hands. Press for a few moments and then remove the cooled plastic from the stamp.

6. Use your finger to rub metallic paste to the raised relief of the pieces and spray with acrylic sealer to protect the finish.

7. To make tags, stamp words on the plastic using permanent ink. Cut around the words to make rectangle shapes. Punch a hole in one end of each. Shrink the tags and seal with acrylic spray.

8. Connect the shapes using copper wire. To begin, bend the wire about 3 inches from the end into a 90-degree angle using chain-nose or flat-nose pliers.

shrink art jewelry

9. Form a loop by bending the wire in the opposite direction with round-nose pliers.

10. Add one of the bracelet pieces. Clip off the end of the wire about ¼ inch from the loop and bend the short end the wire out to keep the loop formed.

11. Make another loop in the longer end of the wire and add another bracelet piece. Wrap the wire around a few times, hiding the clipped wire. When you have finished connecting all of the bracelet pieces with wrapped loops, add a lobster claw clasp and large jump ring to either end using wrapped wire. Hang the word tags from the bracelet using a small jump ring.

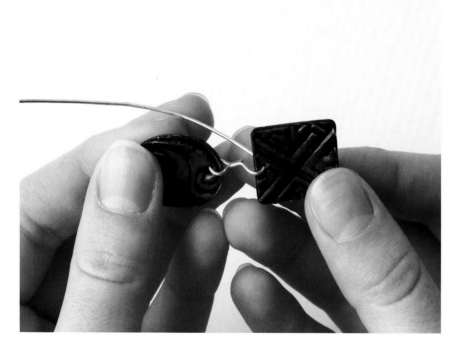

CELTIC EARRINGS

Trace and cut out two slightly smaller circle shapes (about $1\frac{1}{2}$ inches across) to make earrings. Punch a hole at the top and one at the bottom of each circle. Follow the bracelet instructions for shrinking and finishing the pieces. Use a head pin to make a bead dangle to hang from each earring. Hang the earrings from ear wires.

CELTIC PENDANT

To make a Celtic pendant, trace and cut out a larger circle of shrink plastic (about $2\frac{1}{2}$ inches across). Punch a hole at the top for hanging and one or more holes at the bottom for dangles. Shrink the plastic and finish as directed for the bracelet. Use head pins to hang dangles from the bottom holes in the pendant. Hang the pendant from a cord or chain to complete the necklace.

shrink
hearts

Cutting free-form heart shapes gives these charming hearts a whimsical style. Look through your rubber stamp collection for patterns and textures to use on the shrink plastic. You don't need the whole stamp to make a great texture on the hearts; sometimes the most interesting designs are made with just a portion of the stamp design.

YOU WILL NEED FOR TWELVE TO FIFTEEN HEARTS

Frosted Ruff N' Ready Shrinky Dinks plastic

400-grit sandpaper

Lumiere® Paints (Jacquard)

Scissors

Sponge brush for paints

3/16- or 1/4-inch round hole punch

Embossing heat tool

Rubber stamps with various textures (Magenta Style and Aspen Art Stamps)

Rub-On Metallic Highlights paste in copper (Bright Colors set; National Artcraft Co.)

Matte acrylic spray sealer

Gold leafing pen

1. Sand the smooth side of the shrink plastic with sandpaper. Use the sponge brush to coat both sides of the plastic with a thin layer of paint.

2. Draw and cut out heart shapes (see templates on page 124) and punch a hole at the top of each.

3. Use a heat gun to shrink heart shapes one at a time.

4. As soon as the heart has finished shrinking and flattens back down, press a rubber stamp onto the hot plastic. Press firmly with your weight centered over the stamp. Soften the points of the hearts by sanding them a little until smooth and rounded.

5. Apply metallic rub-ons with your finger to the raised relief. Spray heart with acrylic sealer to protect the finish. Color around the edge of the heart with gold leafing pen if desired. Attach jump rings and hang the hearts from a charm bracelet or a necklace.

polymer clay
jewelry

Making jewelry with polymer clay does not require special skills or equipment. Polymer clay is a versatile medium that can be used to make small jewelry elements like beads or large solid pieces like bangle bracelets, and it is perfect for both bold contemporary designs and pieces that mimic antiques.

Polymer clay is a colorful,

oven-curing clay that is available in craft and hobby stores. Polymer clay is made of particles of polyvinyl chloride (PVC), to which a plasticizer has been added to make the material flexible. In addition to all colors of the rainbow, polymer clay comes in metallic gold, silver, bronze, and pearl. There are also translucent and liquid forms of polymer clay. It can be modified to imitate stone, ivory, glass, or metal, and images can be transferred to it. Polymer clay can also be combined with paint, metal leaf, pigment powders, and other materials.

Although not mandatory for working with polymer clay, a pasta roller or acrylic rod or roller, a needle tool or awl, a tissue blade, and clay cutters will help give your finished pieces a professional look.

Polymer clay must be conditioned, by kneading it with your hands until soft. After conditioning the clay, you can sculpt, roll, or shape it any way you like. A favorite tool of polymer clay artists is a pasta roller. Pasta rollers produce nice even sheets of clay in varying thicknesses. All tools used with polymer clay should be dedicated only for that use. Polymer clay should not come into contact with any food-handling items.

To cure polymer clay, bake it on a glass baking dish, ceramic tile, or clean piece of plain white paper placed on a baking pan or cookie sheet. Most polymer clay brands can be baked at 275°F for 30 minutes. Polymer clay emits toxic fumes if fired above the temperature given by the manufacturer. For those who work with polymer clay frequently, it's best to use a toaster oven dedicated to polymer clay. Baking fuses the clay particles into a durable plastic. When properly fused, the clay remains flexible after baking. Let the clay cool in the oven for a stronger finished product.

The baked clay can be carved, sanded, buffed, or left as is. Sanding and buffing create a smooth surface. Use wet/dry sandpaper, rinsing it frequently to prevent dust buildup. Start with 320- or 400-grit sandpaper, moving up to 600-grit paper. For more shine, work up to 800- and 1000-grit papers (available at auto supply stores). Buff the piece on a muslin wheel or with a buffing cloth for a glass-like finish.

candy-stripe
bangle bracelets

Project by: Karen Scudder

These colorful bracelets designed by polymer clay artist Karen Scudder are fun to make and use very little clay. The clay is worked onto memory wire, a very strong, coiled wire that snaps back to its original shape when expanded and released. Memory wire bracelets are comfortable to wear and can be casual or formal depending on the clay colors you choose. Make and wear multiple bracelets in a rainbow of colors, or choose colors based on different holidays: black and orange for Halloween or candy-cane colors for Christmas.

YOU WILL NEED FOR ONE BANGLE

1/2 to 1 oz. polymer clay
(Kato Polyclay™)

Small knitting needle, at least 8 inches long and 1mm in diameter, or unbendable wire, such as music wire

Memory wire
(two to three loops)

Sturdy wire cutters, old pair or from hardware store (jewelry wire cutters are generally not strong enough to cut memory wire)

Tissue blade

Two "E" beads or 4mm glass beads

Round-nose pliers

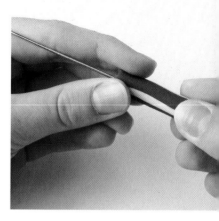

1. Knead the clay to condition and roll a small log about 1 inch long by 1/2 inch thick. Add small thin ropes of contrasting clay around the sides for stripes.

2. Poke the knitting needle through the end of the log, being careful to keep the hole centered.

3. Begin stretching the clay along the needle: Compact the clay firmly to the needle and stretch the clay with your fingers along the needle.

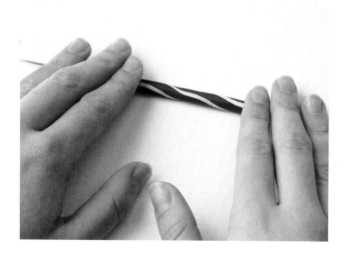

4. Roll the clay gently (on a smooth surface) to make an even rope on the needle. If you roll too vigorously the clay will separate from the needle, trapping air inside. Alternate back and forth between stretching and rolling, keeping the clay compact.

5. Continue to roll and stretch until the rope is 7 to 8 inches long and no more than 1/8 to 3/16 inch in diameter (if it is wider the clay may break as you put it on the memory wire). The stripes will form a nice spiral design if you twist the clay as you roll. Bake on a piece of paper (to avoid a shiny spot) set on a baking pan or cookie sheet at 275°F for 45 minutes.

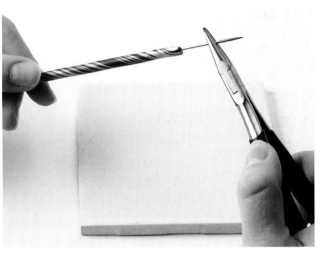

6. Clip a piece of memory wire large enough to fit around your wrist plus a few extra inches with wire cutters. Use caution when you clip as the wire can be very strong and sharp ends can cause injury.

7. Remove the clay tube from the oven, using potholders as the knitting needle may be very hot. Let the piece cool a little. Twist the needle out gently with pliers while the piece is still warm. Trim off the ends of the clay with the tissue blade to make clean ends.

8. String the clay tube onto the memory wire.

9. Add an "E" bead to one end of the tube for an accent and make a loop with the end of the memory wire using the round-nose pliers. Clip off the excess wire. Add a bead and loop to the other end to finish.

faux turquoise
donut pendant

Faux turquoise made with polymer clay looks just like the real thing. You can make large pieces or unusual shapes that would be very expensive or difficult to find in real turquoise. Tory Hughes, an artist working in polymer clay, has developed many imitative techniques. She uses translucent clay, paints, and other materials to modify polymer clays to resemble natural materials, including turquoise, jade, coral, ivory, and amber, to name just a few. This project is a quick modified version of how to make faux turquoise with a few simple tools and materials.

1. Mix two parts turquoise to one part white polymer clay. Add a small amount of raw sienna clay to soften the color and small amounts of sea green and cadmium yellow clay to adjust the color of the turquoise for a greener shade. Let the clay sit until it firms up; you can speed the process by placing the ball of clay in the refrigerator or other very cool place.

2. Break and tear the firm clay into small bits or chunks. Try not to handle the clay too much to avoid softening it.

YOU WILL NEED FOR ONE PENDANT

1 oz. turquoise polymer clay (Premo™)

¹/₂ oz. white polymer clay (Premo)

Small amounts of raw sienna, sea green, cadmium yellow, burnt umber, and black polymer clay (Premo)

³/₈-inch round pattern cutter (Kemper Tools)

Brass wire or head pin

Burnt umber acrylic artist's paint

Baby wipe cloths

320-, 400-, and 600-grit wet/dry sandpaper

Muslin wheel or soft cloth for buffing

Decorating chalks in the following colors: yellow, orange, and light brown (National Artcraft Co.)

Faceted glass bead (for center of donut)

Two small beads (to use at base of head pin for decoration)

Chain-nose and round-nose pliers (for making wire loop at top of pendant)

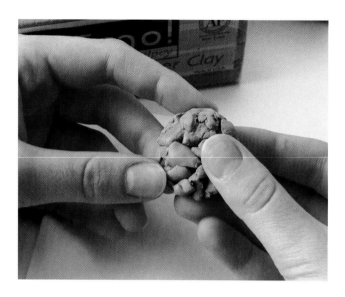

3. Gather the bits of clay and form them into a rough ball. Flatten the ball to make a disk, leaving cracks and irregularities in the clay.

4. Use your fingers to pinch around the edge of the disk to bevel the shape.

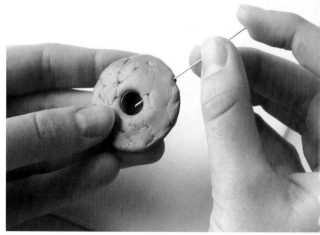

5. Cut out the center with the round cutter.

6. Push a head pin or wire through the clay donut before baking. Leave the pin in place while baking. Place the donut shape on a piece of plain white paper and bake on a glass baking dish or ceramic tile at 275°F for 20 minutes. Let the shape cool in the oven.

7. Mix burnt umber clay with a bit of black clay. Rub the softened clay into the large cracks and pits of the baked donut. Rub acrylic paint into the finer cracks and lines.

8. Wipe off the excess clay and clean with a baby wipe cloth. Bake the clay donut again for 20 minutes at 275°F.

9. Sand the baked donut starting with 320-grit sandpaper. To avoid dust buildup, rinse the dust off the sandpaper as you sand. Work with progressively finer sandpaper under water until the clay is smooth. Finish by buffing on a muslin wheel or by hand with a soft cloth until the clay surface is shiny.

10. Rub yellow, orange, or light brown chalk onto the surface to add depth of color to the turquoise. Real turquoise varies in color, so use more than one color on the same donut. Bake again for another 10 minutes at 275°F to set the chalk.

polymer clay jewelry

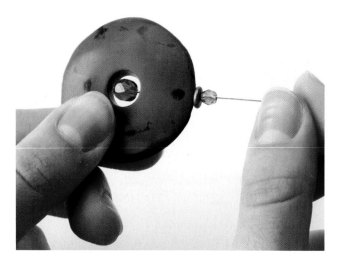

11. Remove the head pin or wire and add beads to the bottom for decoration. Push the head pin or wire through a bead in the center of the donut. Form a loop at the top for hanging (see steps 1 and 2 on page 24). You can hang the necklace from a chain or create a chain by linking stones and beads together using loops formed with brass wire. Add a lobster claw clasp and a jump ring to the last link on each end to join.

TURQUOISE BRACELET

To make a turquoise bracelet, follow steps 1 and 2 of the instructions for making the donut pendant. After breaking the firm clay in step 2, form the clay

into small nuggets. Roll the nuggets into irregular rock shapes and use a needle tool to make a hole through each nugget. Bake the nuggets and add burnt umber clay, paint, and colored chalk as directed for the pendant. The nuggets are small and difficult to sand, so omit the sanding and instead buff with a soft cloth after the second baking. String the nuggets with purchased glass beads and semiprecious stones onto nylon-coated wire using crimp beads and a loop-and-toggle clasp.

asian-style
floral pendant

Project by: Jacqueline Lee

Jacqueline Lee is an artist with a talent for precision and detail. Her pieces show fine craftsmanship in structure and design. Multiple bakings and precise cutting methods are the secret to creating her refined looking jewelry. This project uses Lazertran Silk waterslide decal paper to transfer images onto polymer clay. This paper is designed to be used with toner-based inks, which are commonly used in copy machines. The toner is transferred and baked onto the surface of the clay, enabling you to make colorful jewelry pieces from your favorite images.

YOU WILL NEED FOR ONE PENDANT

Images copied on Lazertran Silk (using toner-based copier)

1/4 oz. white polymer clay (Premo)

1/4 oz. ecru polymer clay (Premo)

Pasta roller or acrylic rod

Tissue blade

Nail file or fine sandpaper

1/2 oz. black polymer clay (Premo)

Two eye pins

Wire cutters (for clipping eye pins)

Chain-nose pliers (for bending eye pins)

Craft knife (for scoring clay)

Kato Clear Polyclay medium

Brush for medium

Toothpick or wooden skewer

Cornstarch

Two 6-inch pieces of white crochet or craft cord

White glue (Sobo)

24- to 30-inch black cord for hanging pendant

Decorative bead with large hole

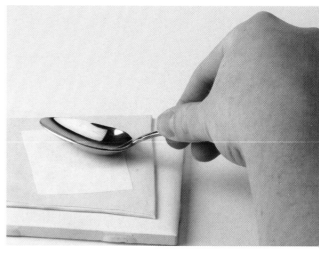

1. Print desired image on Lazertran Silk, following manufacturer's instructions. Cut out the image, leaving a border around the design.

2. Mix two parts white clay to one part ecru to make ivory-colored clay. Roll the clay through the pasta roller on setting #4 (into a thin sheet if rolling by hand). Cut a small square from the sheet and place on a smooth ceramic tile. Burnish the Lazertran image facedown on the surface of the clay, using your fingers or the back of a spoon. Let the clay and transfer sit for 30 minutes.

3. Place the tile and clay into a shallow pan of water for about 2 to 3 minutes until the paper separates and floats away from the image.

4. Remove the clay from the water and gently pat the surface to absorb the moisture. Trim the design using a tissue blade; this pendant was cut into a rectangle. Bake the piece at 275°F for 10 minutes. Sand the edges to round off corners using a nail file or fine sandpaper.

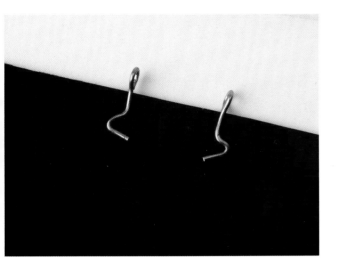

5. Roll out a thick sheet of black clay (#1 or thickest setting on the pasta roller). Lay the sheet on a tile. Trim a clean edge along the top of the clay. Clip and use pliers to bend the bottom of the eye pins (perpendicular to the eye). Place them at the top edge of the clay and press them into the clay.

6. Score the back of the baked piece with a craft knife. Apply Kato medium with a brush to the back of the piece.

7. Press the baked layer onto the unbaked black layer.

8. Trim away the excess black clay with the tissue blade. If you want a border around the image, use a toothpick or wooden skewer as a guide for cutting around the edge. Set the pendant aside.

9. To make the clay hairpipe bead, roll a small ball of clay and stick a toothpick or wooden skewer that has been dusted with cornstarch through it. Roll the ball into a small cylinder on the toothpick.

10. Roll the end of each side of the clay cylinder to taper. Bake the pendant and the hairpipe bead for 30 minutes at 275°F.

11. While it's still warm, use the tissue blade to trim off the rough ends of the hairpipe bead and cut it to size.

12. String one piece of the crochet or craft thread through the eye pin in front of the hairpipe bead. Bring both ends of the cord back over the hairpipe and bring one end through the eye pin again on the back side of the bead.

13. Tie the ends of the cord in a square knot in the back. Clip and glue to secure. Repeat on the other side.

14. Attach a cord for hanging the pendant by tying a lark's head knot over the hairpipe bead. To make a knot, fold the cord in half to form a loop. Wrap the loop around the hairpipe and thread the ends of the cord through the loop. Add a bead over both cords and slide into place above the knot. Knot the cord to finish.

JAPANESE WOODCUT PIN

To make a pin, apply a Lazertran image to polymer clay as described in steps 1 through 4 of the pendant instructions. Roll out a thick sheet (#1 on the pasta roller) of black polymer clay, score the back of the baked piece, and use Kato Polyclay medium to attach the pieces. Trim the edges of the black clay flush with the baked piece or leave a border. Bake the pin at 275°F for 30 minutes. Sand the edges with a nail file to smooth. Attach a pin back using Sobo white

glue, making sure the hinge is on the right. Cut out a rectangle of very thin black clay the width of the inside of the pin back and about 1/2 inch tall. Brush a film of Kato medium above and below where the pin back is glued to the clay. Place the clay rectangle over the area and press to adhere. Bevel the edge of the rectangle with a needle tool for a more finished look. Bake the piece image side down on a perfectly clean tile or sheet of white paper for 10 minutes at 275°F.

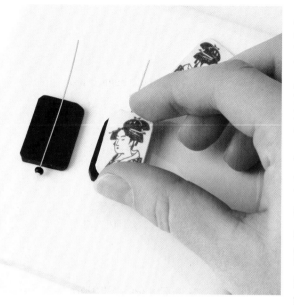

JAPANESE WOODCUT EARRINGS

Follow steps 1 through 4 of the pendant instructions to apply images to polymer clay (two mirror images). Roll out a thick sheet (#1 on the pasta roller) of black polymer clay. Lightly place the baked pieces on the clay and use them as a guide to cut two rectangles from the black clay, and then lift off the baked pieces. Add one glass "E" bead to each of two head pins. Center one head pin onto each piece of black clay. Score the back of the baked pieces and use Kato Polyclay medium to attach them over the head pins, pressing onto the black clay rectangles. Bake the earrings at 275°F for 30 minutes. Sand the edges with a nail file to smooth. Clip and bend the head pins into loops at the top of each earring and hang on ear wires to finish.

gold-stamped kanji
pendant

Project by: Jacqueline Lee

Stamping a kanji, or Japanese pictogram, in gold bronzing powder creates a striking image for this elegant pendant. This project involves several layers and multiple bakings. The instructions are written in order of assembly, but it may be helpful to read through the steps and create all of the clay layers first, and then assemble and bake the layers. Wear a painter's mask when working with the gold bronzing powder; you do not want to breathe the fine particles as you work.

YOU WILL NEED FOR ONE PENDANT

$^1/_2$ oz. black polymer clay (Premo)

Pasta roller

Craft knife

Two Asian-style rubber stamps (large kanji character and background pattern stamp)

Gold bronzing powder

$^1/_2$ oz. copper polymer clay (Premo)

Gold metal leaf or composition leaf

Kato Clear Polyclay medium

Brush for medium

Tissue blade

Two eye pins

Wire cutters (for clipping eye pins)

Chain-nose pliers (for bending eye pins)

Last six supplies listed on page 81

polymer clay jewelry

1. Layer #1: Roll a thin sheet of black clay on setting #4 of the pasta roller. Rub bronzing powder on the kanji stamp and stamp onto the clay. Cut out a circle shape around the stamped image with the craft knife and bake the circle on a glass baking dish or tile at 275°F for 10 minutes. Set aside.

2. Layer #2: Roll out a sheet of copper clay on setting #3 of the pasta roller and trim it to a 2-inch square. Lay this square facedown on gold leaf (the leaf will stick to it) and trim leaf with the tissue blade to fit.

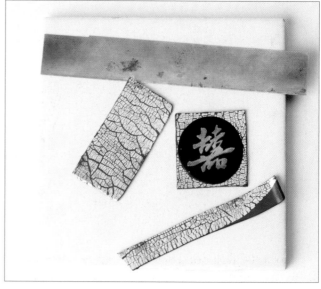

3. Roll the clay and gold leaf through the pasta roller on setting #3 to adhere leaf. Run the sheet through again on setting #4 to crackle the leaf. Turn the clay a quarter turn and run the sheet through again on setting #5.

4. Score the back of the baked circle kanji piece (layer #1) with a craft knife. Brush on a coat of Kato Polyclay medium, and press onto the copper/gold leaf layer (layer #2). Trim the copper clay into a square with the tissue blade to frame the kanji circle. Bake on a glass baking dish or tile at 275°F for 10 minutes.

5. Layer #3: Roll a sheet of black clay through the pasta roller on setting #5 and set it on the tile or baking dish that you will be baking it on later. (Placing the clay on the tile or dish helps to keep it from moving and distorting the image.) Rub bronzing powder on the Asian pattern stamp and stamp onto clay.

6. After the baked layers (#1 and #2) have cooled, score the back of the baked kanji piece with a knife and brush with the Kato medium. Press onto the black clay with the Asian pattern stamped onto it (layer #3). Using the tissue blade, trim the sides flush with the top layers, leaving a narrow border on the top and bottom.

7. Layer #4: Roll out a sheet of copper clay on setting #1 of the pasta roller. Trim the top of the sheet with the tissue blade and press bent eye pins into the clay (see step 5 of the Asian-style floral pendant project on page 83). Score the back of the three-layer assemblage and brush with the Kato medium. Press onto the copper clay. Trim this layer as you did layer #3 in step 6.

8. Create a hairpipe bead as directed in steps 9 through 11 of the floral pendant project. Bake the finished pendant and hairpipe bead at 275°F for 30 minutes. To complete the necklace, add a cord as directed in steps 12 through 14 of the floral pendant project.Use a purchased bead to slide over the cords or make a bead using the leftover copper clay and gold leaf. Use a skewer to make a large hole in the bead and bake at 275°F for 30 minutes.

polymer clay jewelry

mica pearl
pendant

Pearlescent polymer clays contain small reflective particles of mica. As the clay is rolled the mica particles become flattened and line up on the surface of the clay, making them more reflective. The clay becomes brighter with a pearly sheen on the surface. Underneath the surface the clay is darker and less brilliant. In this project the clay is imprinted with a rubbing plate to create a relief pattern. Slicing a blade across the surface to remove the raised portions reveals the contrast between the layers and creates an interesting holographic effect. The surface is perfectly flat yet appears to be three-dimensional.

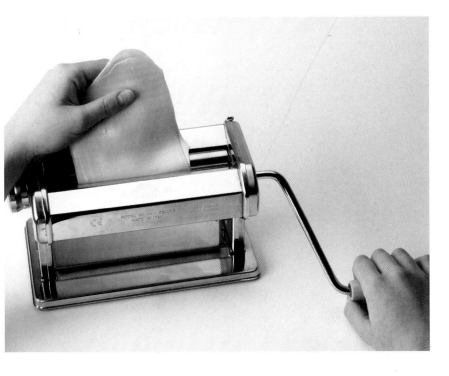

YOU WILL NEED FOR ONE PENDANT

1 oz. white pearl, red pearl, or gold polymer clay (Premo)

Pasta roller

Shade-Tex® Rubbing Plate (Scratch-Art® Co. Inc.)

Talc or baby powder

Acrylic rod or smooth drinking glass to roll clay

Tissue blade

Craft knife

Template or paper pattern

3/4-inch round pattern cutter (Kemper Tools)

Small copied images

White decoupage glue

Brush for glue

20-gauge half-hard silver wire

Chain-nose and round-nose pliers

Wire cutters

Epoxy resin (Envirotex Lite)

1. Roll a sheet of pearl polymer clay through the thickest setting (#1) on the pasta roller. Roll the clay through the pasta roller at least ten times, folding the sheet in half on each pass. For the final pass, roll the sheet on setting #3 to make it thinner. Fold the sheet in half and place on a smooth, flat work surface.

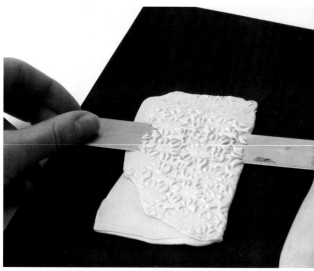

2. Dust the sheet of clay and the rubbing plate with talc or baby powder to prevent the clay from sticking. Place the texture sheet on the surface of the clay and roll across it with the acrylic rod or glass to make a relief pattern. Place the sheet in a refrigerator or other cool area to firm.

3. Skim the surface of the clay with the tissue blade to remove the raised relief of the pattern. Bend the blade slightly to slice off any little missed areas on the surface. A ghost image of the pattern will remain.

4. Roll the surface with the acrylic rod or glass, rolling with just enough pressure to make the surface perfectly level and smooth.

5. Cut out a shape with a craft knife. For the pendant, use a template or paper pattern to make the shape and cut a hole in the center with the round pattern cutter to frame the picture. You can use a different pattern cutter to make a square hole in the middle, as shown for the red pendant.

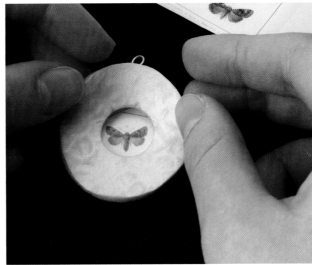

6. Roll the leftover clay through the pasta roller on setting #3 to make a thin sheet of clay for the base piece. Cut a shape using the same pattern or template from step 5. Cut out a small image and brush both sides of the image with white glue to seal. Place the image onto the base clay. Make a wire loop with pliers to hang the pendant (see steps 1 and 2 on page 24). Make a small bend in the wire to keep the hook embedded in the clay. Press this gently onto the top of the base shape.

7. Position the patterned clay over the image so that the hole frames the image. Press the clay to adhere to the back or base clay, sandwiching the image and the hook in between. Bake the piece at 275°F for 30 minutes. You can bake the piece on a glass baking dish or on a piece of plain paper placed on a cookie sheet. Baking on paper prevents a shiny surface on the back of the baked piece. Let the piece cool in the oven.

8. Mix the epoxy resin according to the manufacturer's instructions and coat the image with a layer of epoxy. Let the epoxy dry overnight or for several days undisturbed in a warm place. Hang the pendant from a cord or chain.

resin
jewelry

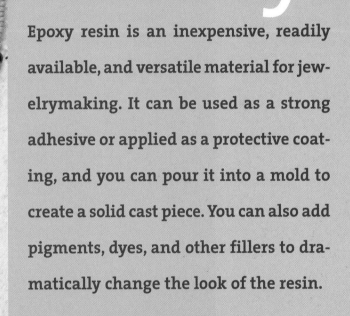

Epoxy resin is an inexpensive, readily available, and versatile material for jewelrymaking. It can be used as a strong adhesive or applied as a protective coating, and you can pour it into a mold to create a solid cast piece. You can also add pigments, dyes, and other fillers to dramatically change the look of the resin.

Epoxy resin is a two-part mixture of resin and a catalyst (hardener).

When mixed together, the resin and the catalyst create a reaction that allows the resin to begin curing. The finished product is a crystal-clear hard plastic. Epoxy resin was originally formulated to be used as an adhesive or clear protective coating. As an adhesive, it works very well on non-porous surfaces. It is also commonly applied to floors and tabletops to create a clear waterproof laminate. In addition to surface treatments, some recently developed formulas of epoxy resin can be poured into molds to make solid cast pieces.

As a jewelrymaking medium, epoxy resin can be used in a variety of ways:

- Use resin as a protective coating to simulate glass or plastic.
- Encase fragile items such as dried flowers, miniatures, hard candy, or seashells in resin.
- Pour resin into molds to make solid jewelry charms or pendants.
- Fill bezels or metal stampings with resin to simulate glass enamel.

Epoxy resin is inexpensive, and several brands are available through jewelry suppliers and craft stores. Envirotex Lite, Colores™, and Devcon 2-Ton Clear Epoxy are just a few of the most common brands on the market. Some brands have color added to the resin, while some are clear.

Epoxy resin can be mixed with other materials to create different effects. You can add color to the resin in the form of pigments or dyes. Add a little pigment or dye to create a translucent color; add more for an opaque mixture. Try mixing or layering the resin with materials such as glitter, sand, gold or silver leaf, paper, rhinestones, or beads. Liquids, such as oil paints, may react with the resin, so it is best to stick with dry materials.

The proportions for mixing epoxy resin vary from brand to brand. Make sure you mix the epoxy resin thoroughly and follow the manufacturer's instructions carefully for success. When working with epoxy resin, be sure to read all of the manufacturer's instructions and safety warnings carefully. Always work in a well-ventilated area. Avoid contact with your skin and eyes by wearing gloves and eye protection. Follow the proper procedures as indicated on the package and avoid extreme temperatures when storing resin.

cast resin heart pendant

This project uses epoxy resin especially formulated for casting. This resin can be tinted, colored, or combined with other materials, such as glitter, granite powders, and metal leaf. There are molds designed to be used with the resin, or you can make your own molds using a latex rubber known as Mold Builder. Using mold release spray facilitates successful release of the resin from the molds.

YOU WILL NEED FOR ONE PENDANT

Castin'Craft molds or Soap Gems molds (ETI)

Mold release spray

EasyCast Clear Casting Epoxy (ETI)

Plastic measure/mixing cup

Wooden stir stick

Red and yellow Castin'Craft Transparent Dyes (ETI)

Suze Weinberg's Ultra Effects in silver (Ranger)

Suze Weinberg's BeaDazzles in "Jazz" (Ranger)

Plasticine (children's modeling clay)

Nail file

26-gauge orange wire (Artistic Wire)

Twelve 6mm orange AB crystals

Twelve 6mm fuchsia crystals

Twenty-four each of orange and pink size 10/0 or 11/0 seed beads

Chain-nose and round-nose pliers

Wire cutters

1. Prepare mold by spraying with mold release according to package instructions. Let the mold dry thoroughly.

2. Follow manufacturer's instructions carefully to mix casting epoxy in a plastic cup (5cc each resin and hardener for small batch). Measure carefully and stir thoroughly. Add a drop of yellow dye and a small drop of red dye to the mixture and continue stirring.

3. Stir in Ultra Effects and BeaDazzles sprinkles.

4. Stick a bit of plasticine clay to the side of the mold to create a depression in which the wire will later sit. Pour the mixed EasyCast epoxy resin into the prepared mold. Let the resin in the mold cure in a warm place (between 70°F and 85°F) for 24 hours until the resin is hard.

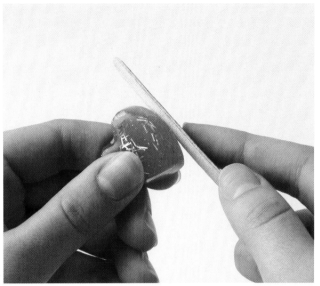

5. To remove the piece from the mold, press on the sides and push the back of the mold until the piece falls out. Place the mold in the freezer for about 15 minutes if the piece is difficult to remove.

6. Sand the edges of the cast piece with a nail file.

7. Remove the plasticine with a toothpick.

8. Bend a 12-inch piece of wire in half and twist the strands together. Place the twisted wire in the depression and fill with a bit more resin. Prop up the piece to prevent the resin from flowing out until the piece dries. Twist or wrap the wires to make a loop on the top of the cast piece. To make a necklace, wrap beads with orange wire and join together (see steps 1 through 5 on pages 24 and 25).

bottle cap pins
and pendants

The charm and whimsy of jewelry made from found objects is the surprise of the unexpected. Everyday objects that are often overlooked or discarded can be transformed into glittering jewels. Bezels are defined as a rim that encompasses a jewel or other object. You can make a bezel out of anything that fits this definition. Bottle caps make the perfect bezel for nostalgia-themed jewelry pins and pendants. You can recycle caps you have lying around or purchase them inexpensively from brewery suppliers or online.

1. Glue vintage images onto cardstock paper using white glue or glue stick. Punch out circles with hole punch or cut using a 1-inch circle template.

YOU WILL NEED FOR SEVERAL PINS OR PENDANTS

Vintage images from clip art books or collage sheets

Cardstock paper

White glue

1-inch round hole punch (optional)

Decoupage glue (Mod Podge)

Brush for decoupage glue

Drill or pin vise with 1/16-inch drill bit (for making holes in caps for pendant or dangles)

Bottle caps (ARTchix Studio; Beer Nut)

Rhinestones, glitter, beads, and other small found objects

Jump rings for pendant or dangles

Two-part epoxy resin (Envirotex Lite)

Plastic measure/mixing cup

Wooden stir stick

Pin back findings (for pins)

Beads or charms (optional)

Head pins and eye pins for pendants or dangles (optional)

Ball chain (for hanging pendant)

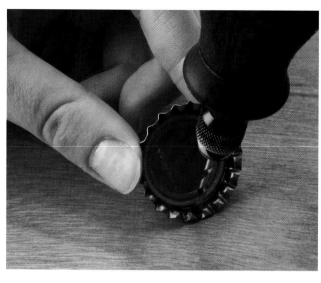

2. Brush both sides of circle shapes with decoupage glue, then let dry.

3. Drill holes in the bottle caps if you want to make necklaces or add hanging elements.

4. Glue the circles into the caps with a small drop of white glue applied to the back of the circle. Use white glue to attach rhinestones, beads, or glitter to embellish the images. Let the glue dry thoroughly.

5. Add jump rings at this step if desired. Cover the holes with clear tape on the outside of the caps after attaching jump rings to keep the resin (added in step 6) from leaking out.

6. Mix epoxy resin with the wooden stir stick in the plastic cup according to the manufacturer's instructions. Mix well to insure proper curing. Coat each image with the epoxy until the cap is about half full. After about 5 minutes, air bubbles caused by stirring rise to the surface. Gently exhale over the surface to release the bubbles. Do not inhale. Let the epoxy dry in a warm place (between 70°F and 80°F), undisturbed, overnight or until surface is no longer tacky.

7. Glue on pin backs with epoxy or use self-adhesive pin back findings. Attach beads to jump rings with head pins and eye pins if desired. For a pendant omit the pin back finding and hang the cap from a ball chain.

resin jewelry

pressed flower pendant
& earrings

Floral patterns have been a popular theme for jewelry design since ancient times. In this project brightly colored flowers combine with contrasting polymer clay to create a contemporary, fashionable look. Pressed flowers can be found in craft stores or you can press your own. For a softer, more old-fashioned style, try using light or pastel polymer clay colors for the backgrounds. Look through your wardrobe or floral fabrics for inspiration.

YOU WILL NEED FOR ONE PENDANT OR PAIR OF EARRINGS

Wire or eye pins

Chain-nose and flat-nose pliers

Wire cutters

$1/4$ oz. or small ball of polymer clay (Premo)

Pasta roller or acrylic rod

Clay cutters or small cookie cutters (ovals and circles)

Decoupage glue (Mod Podge)

Brush for glue

Pressed flowers (Nature's Pressed)

Tweezers to lift flowers

Aluminum foil

Foam tape

Two-part epoxy resin (Envirotex Lite)

Toothpicks

Two ear wires (for earrings)

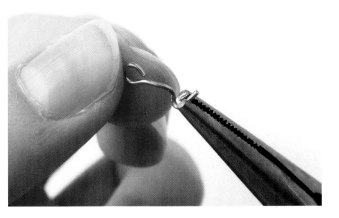

1. You will need to make wire loops out of wire or eye pins for hanging the pendant or attaching ear wires (see steps 1 and 2 on page 24 for instructions on making wire loops). Make a bend in the wire to keep it from pulling out of the clay. (If you're making earrings, make loops at the top and bottom—one for attaching the ear wire and one for hanging a dangle.)

2. Condition polymer clay by kneading it until soft. Roll the clay through the pasta roller on setting #1, or to $1/8$ inch thick if using an acrylic rod. Cut out shapes with cutters and push the wire loop into the top of the clay.

3. Bake the shapes in the oven at 275°F for 20 minutes on a glass baking dish or ceramic tile. Place the shapes on a piece of plain white paper if you want to avoid a shiny surface on the back of the clay. Let the shapes cool in the oven. Brush the shapes with a thin layer of decoupage glue.

4. Carefully place the flowers on the baked clay shapes and gently press to adhere. It helps to use tweezers to lift and place the flowers.

resin jewelry

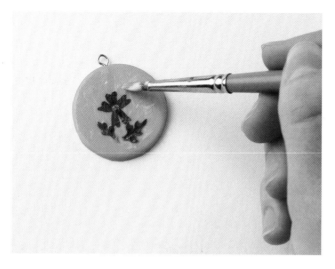

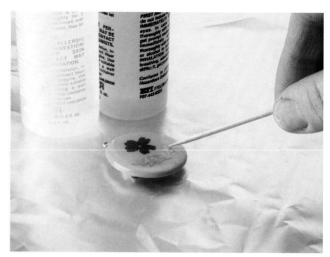

5. Gently brush the flowers with another layer of glue. Let the glue dry.

7. Use a jump ring to attach the pendant to a beaded necklace, or attach ear wires to wire loops to make earrings. If you want to hang bead dangles, add another wire loop at the bottom of the shape in step 1. String beads on head pins and attach to loops with wrapped wire loops (see steps 1 through 3 on page 24).

6. Cover a flat surface with aluminum foil. Set the shapes on squares of foam tape to keep them suspended and level. Mix epoxy according to manufacturer's instructions. Apply a small amount in the center of each piece, using a toothpick to coat the surface and edges. Let the pieces dry undisturbed in a warm area (between 70°F and 80°F).

PRESSED FLOWER BRACELET

To make a pressed flower bracelet, cut small pieces of black or white paper to fit in each bracelet bezel. Coat both sides of the paper pieces with decoupage glue. Glue the pieces down into each bezel on the bracelet. Place the flowers onto each section. Coat with decoupage glue and let the glue dry. Mix the epoxy according to manufacturer's instructions. Mix well to insure proper curing. Fill each bezel with epoxy to cover the flowers, using a toothpick to coax the epoxy into the corners and around the edges. Let the epoxy dry in a warm place (between 70°F and 80°F) overnight.

YOU WILL NEED FOR ONE BRACELET

Silver rectangle bracelet (ARTchix Studio)

White or black paper for backgrounds

Scissors

Decoupage glue (Mod Podge)

Brush for glue

Pressed flowers (Nature's Pressed)

Two-part epoxy (Envirotex Lite)

Toothpicks

retro picture
jewelry

The technology to copy and transfer images to various surfaces and the wide range of new art materials on the market make it possible to create miniature works of wearable art. By choosing fun retro images, you can fashion jewelry that is casual or whimsical, and that expresses your personality.

Retro picture jewelry

Retro picture jewelry is fun and easy to make. To get started, all you have to do is find some great images you'd like to use. Copyright-free images can be found from a number of sources. Dover Publications carries books and CD-ROMs of copyright-free images organized by subject. There are ephemera collections and sources on the Internet for vintage images. Look through your own collection of old books, recipes, and photos to find images that can be copied and used to make jewelry.

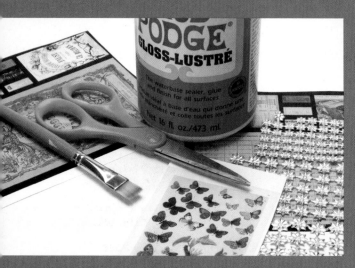

All you need to start making picture jewelry is scissors, glue, and an assortment of fun images.

New technologies make it easier than ever to incorporate images into jewelry designs. Color copiers, scanners, photo-manipulation software, and ink jet printers enable you to size, retouch, and print images to your exact specifications. You can use photo transfer papers to print an image with your ink jet printer and apply it to fabric, leather, wood, or any other porous surface.

The basic supplies for working with paper images are a good pair of stainless steel scissors and glue. You can use white glue or decoupage glue, such as Mod Podge, which seals paper to protect the surface and is available in matte or gloss. Epoxy resin will give your piece a durable, glass-like finish. Gem or jewel glue is useful for attaching small items, such as beads and rhinestones, to your piece. Paper punches in different sizes and shapes are not mandatory, but can make it much easier to cut out clean, even shapes.

You may want to collect small items and memorabilia to embellish your jewelry and give it a vintage look. Miniature shops and hobby shops are great sources for small objects. Thrift stores are also a great source for broken jewelry to recycle.

Think about the style of the piece you are making when choosing images to use. If the piece you are designing involves multiple images, you may want to choose images that follow a theme or mix them up for a more eclectic look. You can also combine multiple images into a collage.

leather
bracelet

This fun project involves transferring an image to leather using T-shirt transfer paper, which is widely available at office supply stores. Transfer paper for dark T-shirts is opaque, and negative space around the image will be white. Standard T-shirt paper is transparent in the negative space around the image, allowing the color of the leather to show through. You can dress up the finished pieces by gluing embellishments, such as rhinestones and beads, to the leather using jewel glue or by painting the leather with acrylic paints or fabric paints.

YOU WILL NEED FOR ONE BRACELET

Vintage color images or collage sheets (DMD, Inc. Paper Reflections® Line; Collage Collection by Art Accentz™; Dover Publications)

Ink Jet Dark T-shirt Transfers (Avery®)

Scissors

Leather shears

Small piece of 4- to 5-oz. vegetable-tanned tooling leather (leather and leather-working supplies available through The Leather Factory)

3- to 4mm round leather hole punch

Loop-and-toggle clasp

18- to 20-inch piece of 2mm round leather cord

24-inch piece of 26- or 28-gauge, dead-soft sterling silver wire

Wire cutters and chain-nose pliers

1. Scan and print images onto T-shirt transfer paper, following manufacturer's instructions for printing. Cut out image and peel off paper backing from the transfer.

2. Iron the transfer onto the leather according to manufacturer's instructions.

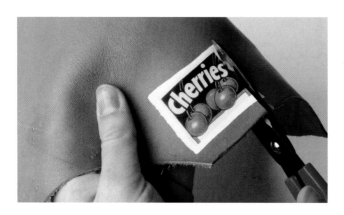

3. Cut out a shape around the image using leather shears (see templates on page 125).

4. Use the leather hole punch to make two small holes on each side of the shape.

LEATHER

Leather is a versatile material for making jewelry. It can be stamped, dyed, painted, or tooled. Leather is very durable, making it great for everyday wear. Leather shops often sell small inexpensive scraps of leather that are the perfect size for making jewelry.

It's helpful to have a few specialized tools when working with leather. Leather shears are very sharp and cut leather easily. Leather punches are necessary for making holes in leather. One type is a steel punch that you place over the leather while you strike it with a mallet. The other type is a handheld rotary punch with a wheel that holds various sizes of punches. Other helpful supplies for leather projects include sets for making snaps, eyelets (small metal rings used to reinforce holes in the leather), and leather lace or cord.

5. Cut the leather cord into two equal pieces, one for each side of the bracelet. To attach cord with a lark's head knot, fold the cord in half to form a loop. Thread the ends of the cord through the holes on one side of the bracelet and bring both through the loop. Pull gently to tighten.

6. Thread the ends of the leather cords through the loop-and-toggle clasp. Adjust the cord to fit around your wrist. Make a "Z" shape with the wire and hold it parallel to the cords.

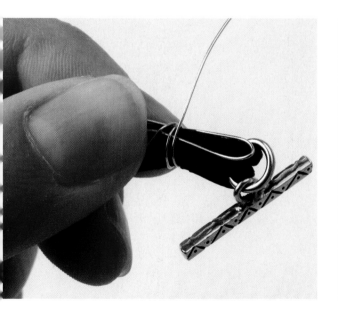

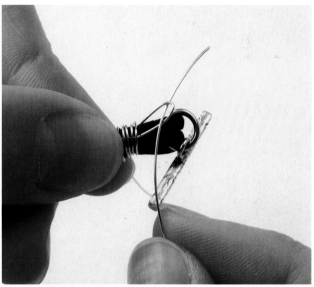

7. Begin wrapping the wire tightly a few times around the cords and the "Z" shape.

8. Bring the end of the wire through the loop on the right as shown.

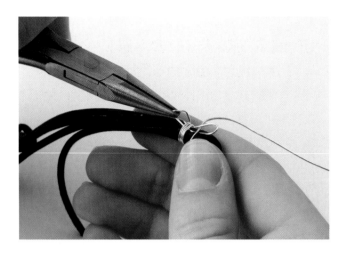

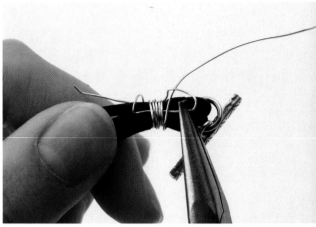

9. Using the chain-nose pliers, twist the wire loop on the left side to keep it from kinking.

10. Tighten the wire wrap by pulling the loop on the right side to "cinch up" the wire loop on the left.

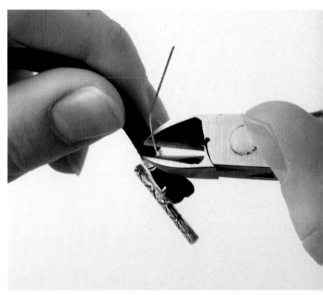

11. Pull the wire on the left side tight to close up the loop on the right side. Pull tightly until the loop disappears under the wire wrapping.

12. Clip the ends of both wires for a neat finish.

13. Trim the ends of the leather cord close to the wrapped wire. Repeat steps 6 through 13 on the other side of the bracelet.

LEATHER PENDANT

Follow steps 1 and 2 of the bracelet instructions to transfer an image to leather. Cut out a shape for the pendant with leather shears (see templates on page 125). Punch a hole at the top, and one at the bottom if you want to add a bead dangle. Make the dangle using a head pin and beads and attach to the bottom hole with a wrapped loop. Make a lark's head knot with leather cord through the top hole for the necklace. Use jump rings to attach a lobster claw clasp to the ends of the cord. Finish the ends of the necklace cord as directed for the leather bracelet using wire to wrap (steps 7 through 13).

LEATHER BARRETTE

Follow the instructions for applying an iron-on transfer to leather as described for the leather bracelet (steps 1 and 2). Cut out a shape for the barrette with leather shears and use Gem-Tac glue or E6000 glue to attach a metal hair clip finding to the leather.

Use clothespins or binder clips to hold the piece while the glue dries.

clear bauble
bracelet

Tiny vintage pictures captured in clear plastic cabochons are the perfect adornment for the young at heart. The clear cabochons magnify even the smallest details of an image. Slide a cabochon over pictures from reduced color copies, magazines, or catalogs to find just the right image to feature. You will be surprised how great even a single alphabet letter looks under the cabochon. For theme bracelets, look through clip art books filled with copyright-free images from the past.

YOU WILL NEED FOR ONE BRACELET

1 oz. black polymer clay (Premo)

Thirteen 15mm clear acrylic cabochons (JonesTones Gem Stones), or for a larger bracelet use ten ³/4-inch cabochons (Industrial Plastics)

Needle tool or awl

Baby wipe cloths

Small images copied on paper or cut from wrapping paper, cards, etc.

¹/2-inch round hole punch (optional)

Scissors

Clear gloss decoupage glue (Mod Podge)

Small brush for glue

E6000 glue

Round black elastic cord

Jewel glue or white glue

1. Condition clay by kneading it thoroughly to soften. Pinch off a bit of clay and roll it into a small marble-size ball. Press a cabochon onto the ball of clay, flattening it until it is about 1/4 inch thick.

2. Roll the clay-backed cabochon on its side to bevel the edge of the clay and to make the clay narrow at the base (this will help the cabochons fit together nicely on the bracelet). Adjust the clay as needed to keep the clay backing no more than 1/4 inch thick. Use this bit of clay as a guide to roll the rest of the balls of clay for the bracelet.

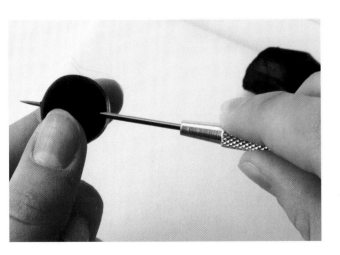

3. Use a needle tool or awl to poke a hole through the clay backing for stringing. Poke through one direction and then the other until the hole goes all the way through the clay.

4. Place the clay-backed cabochons onto a small ceramic tile. Place in the refrigerator or other cool place to firm the clay. Slide the edge of a clean piece of paper in between the cabochon and the clay to separate the pieces without distorting the clay. Set the cabochons aside. Bake the clay pieces on the tile in a preheated oven at 275°F for 20 minutes. Let the pieces cool in the oven. Clean the cabochons with a baby wipe cloth to remove any clay residue.

retro picture jewelry

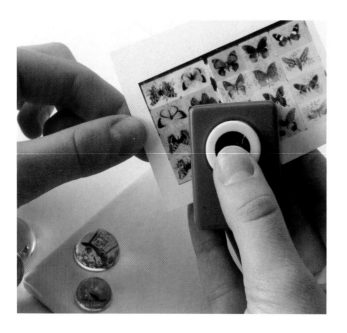

5. Use the hole punch to punch images from paper, or cut them out roughly with scissors.

6. Use the small brush to coat the back of each cabochon with decoupage glue. Brush a thin layer onto each image. Press the image onto the cabochon, smoothing out any air bubbles with your fingers. If using scissors, apply images and trim off excess paper after the glue dries. Coat the back of each cabochon with another layer of decoupage glue to seal the back of the paper. Let the pieces dry.

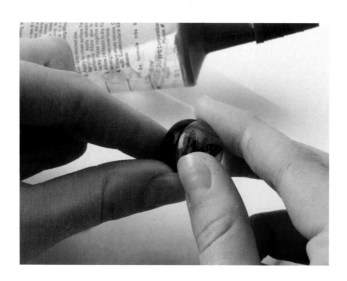

7. Use E6000 glue to attach the cabochons to the clay backings. Let the glue dry overnight.

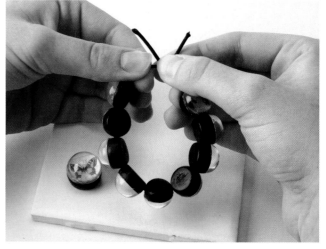

8. String the finished cabochons onto elastic cord. Use the pin vise or drill to enlarge any holes that are too small. Tie the ends with a square knot and clip the excess cord. Apply jewel glue or white glue to the knot to prevent the cord from fraying.

BAUBLE PENDANT

To make a pendant, use a large 1-inch clear cabochon or other desired size. Follow the directions for the bracelet, with the following changes. Instead of using a needle tool or awl to make a hole through the clay for the elastic, insert a head or eye pin (use an eye pin if you want to add a bead dangle) to form a hole in the clay for hanging the pendant. Bake the clay with the pin in place. Make a loop with pliers at the top of the pin to hang the pendant from a chain. If you want to add a dangle, string beads on a head pin and attach the head pin to the loop of the eye pin at the bottom of the pendant.

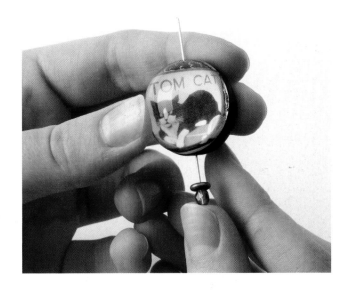

retro picture jewelry

vintage valentine
bracelet

This project makes a valentine that can be worn as jewelry. Copy old photographs or letters or add handwritten messages for a personal touch. You can use other images for different holidays or special events. Small eyelets are used in this project to strengthen the holes for jump rings and to provide a finished look to the jewelry. Eyelets are available wherever scrapbooking supplies are sold. They come in a variety of sizes and finishes. You will need an eyelet setter that matches the size of the eyelet.

YOU WILL NEED FOR ONE BRACELET

Small vintage images (Dover; ARTchix Studio)

Scissors

Glue stick

Two sheets heavy, clear self-laminating adhesive film

Bone folder

1/16-inch hole punch (Fiskars)

1/16-inch micro brass eyelets

Eyelet setter

Self-healing mat

Hammer

3-D Crystal Lacquer (Sakura) or jewel glue

Beads, glitter, rhinestones, etc.

Twelve to fourteen small brass jump rings

Two large brass jump rings for the ends of the bracelet

Gold-toned lobster claw clasp

Brass charms to hang from hearts

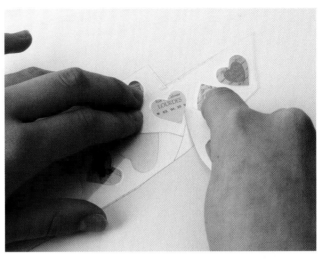

1. Reduce images on color copier to fit small valentine shapes as necessary (see template on page 124). Cut small heart shapes from images. Layer different paper elements to make interesting collages using a glue stick. Add text or personal messages if desired. Peel the protective coating from the laminate sheet. Sandwich the paper hearts in between laminate sheets.

2. Trace around each heart with the bone folder, pressing firmly to adhere the laminate close to the edges.

3. Cut around each shape. If using a laminate with one sticky surface, leave at least a ¹/₈-inch border around each shape to keep the laminate from separating. If using a laminate with one sticky surface. If both sheets are sticky, you can cut right to the edge of the image.

4. Punch a hole on each side of the laminated hearts and on the bottom of any from which you'd like to hang charms.

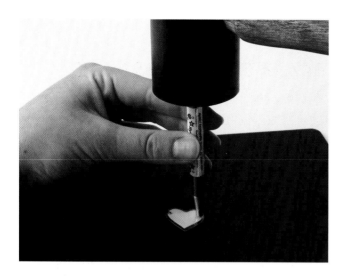

5. Push the eyelets down through the holes, pushing through the side of the heart with the image or design. Hammer the eyelets with the eyelet setter on the self-healing mat.

6. Decorate a few hearts using liquid laminate or jewel glue to attach small beads, rhinestones, gold foil stars, or glitter. Attach small jump rings through the eyelets to link the hearts and to hang charms. Add as many hearts as needed until the bracelet fits around your wrist. Add a large jump ring to one end and a jump ring and lobster claw clasp to the other.

LAMINATE

Office supply and craft stores sell clear laminating film in sheet form. It is available in different weights, varying by brand. Use heavier weights for jewelry projects. Some brands have adhesive on both sides and other types (used to protect documents) have a thick clear plastic top sheet with a thinner adhesive back sheet. You can also use a home laminating machine or go to a copy center to laminate your images.

To laminate images, work on a clean flat surface. The adhesive is very sticky and it's easy to pick up unwanted dust, glitter, or bits of paper. As you smooth the laminate sheets to adhere, it's helpful to use a bone folder (bookbinder's tool) to press around the edges of your images. The bone folder does not scratch the plastic as easily as a metal tool or other hard tool would. You can use a wooden ice cream stick if you do not have a bone folder.

You can laminate paper images, photos, lace, or pressed flowers. For successful lamination, make sure not to build up too much bulk or thickness . If you make a collage you can make a color copy of it and use this copy to laminate. This will allow you to reduce the thickness and you will still have the original to use for future projects.

VALENTINE NECKLACE

To make a pendant, cut out and laminate a larger heart (see template on page 124), following steps 1 through 3 of the bracelet project. Instead of making holes on each side of the heart, make one 1/8-inch hole at the top and one 1/16-inch hole at the bottom. Hammer a larger eyelet through the top and a smaller one through the bottom. Decorate the heart with beads and rhinestones. Add beads to a head pin to create a dangle and attach it to the bottom of the heart with a small jump ring. Hang the heart from a cord or chain with a larger jump ring.

VALENTINE EARRINGS

Make two small laminated hearts (see template on page 124), following the directions for the bracelet. Punch holes and add 1/16-inch eyelets at the top and bottom of each heart. Decorate the hearts with beads and rhinestones and use gold-toned head pins to add beads to dangle from the bottoms of the earrings. Attach the dangles with jump rings. Hang the finished hearts from gold-toned ear wires to complete the earrings.

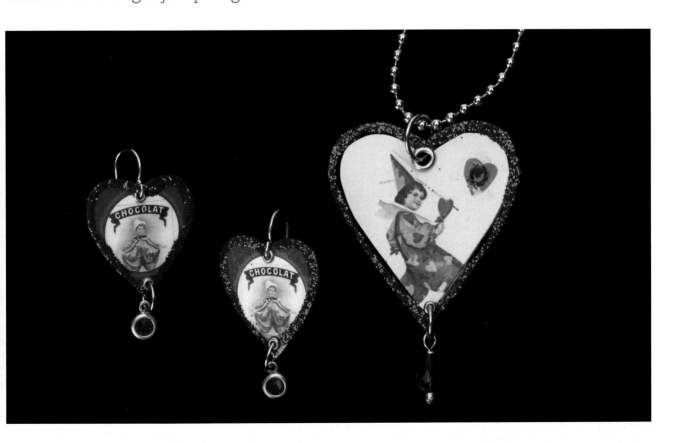

templates

Templates are provided for projects that require tracing and cutting out shapes. The templates are shown full-size and can be photocopied or traced to use. If you would like to try making your own shapes, you can use these templates as a guide for size.

CELTIC KNOTS BRACELET
(Instructions on page 61.)

SHRINK HEARTS
(Instructions on page 66.)

VINTAGE VALENTINE JEWEL
(Instructions on page 120.)

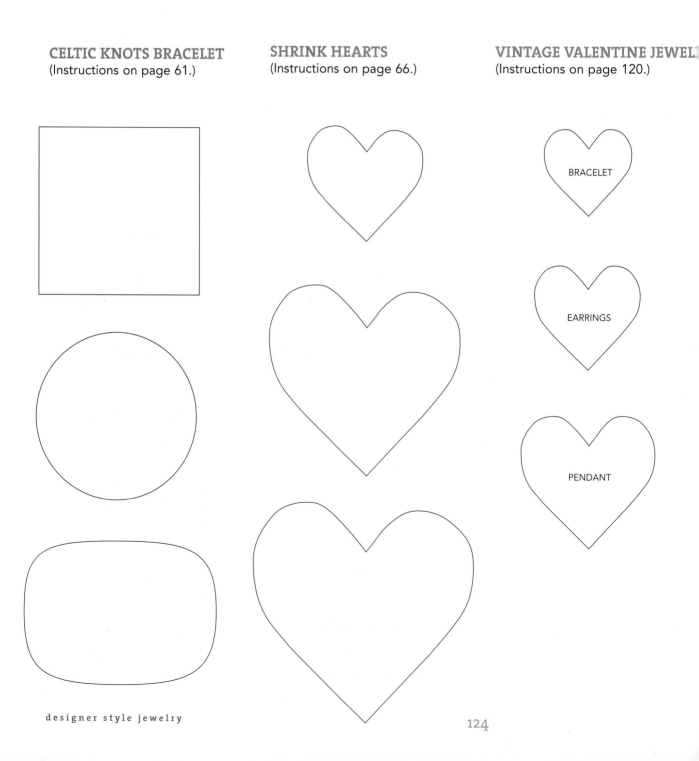

FAUX IVORY SCRIMSHAW PENDANT
(Instructions on page 54.)

LEATHER JEWELRY
(Instructions on page 111.)

VINTAGE PHOTO JEWELRY
(Instructions on page 58. Inside shapes are templates for photos. Outside shapes are templates for backgrounds.)

SMALL PENDANT

SMALL PENDANT

ROUND PENDANT

LARGE PENDANT

LARGE PENDANT

OVAL PENDANT

OVAL BRACELET

EARRINGS

RECTANGULAR BRACELET

suppliers

Listed below are the manufacturers and suppliers of many of the materials used in this book. Most of these companies sell their products to retail and online stores, which are the most dependable source for jewelrymaking supplies. Contact the companies listed directly to find a retailer near you.

ARTchix Studio™
585 Stornoway Drive
Victoria, BC V9C 3L1
CANADA
250-370-9985
www.artchixstudio.com
Vintage collage sheets, charms, fasteners, and findings

Artistic Wire™
752 North Larch Avenue
Elmhurst, IL 60126
630-530-7567
www.artisticwire.com
Wire, tools, and kits

Aspen Art Stamps
www.aspenartstamps.com
Unmounted rubber stamps and stamping supplies

The Bead Shop
158 University Avenue
Palo Alto, CA 94301
650-328-7925
www.beadshop.com
Assorted beads and beading supplies

The Beer Nut
1200 S. State
Salt Lake City, UT 84111
888-825-4697
www.beernut.com
Bottle caps

Blue Moon Beads
7855 Hayvenhurst Avenue
Van Nuys, CA 91406
800-377-6715
www.beads.net
Beads and findings

Clay Factory Inc.
P.O. Box 460598
Escondido, CA 92046-0598
877-728-5739
www.clayfactoryinc.com
Polymer clay, pattern cutters, tools, and general supplies

DMD, Inc. Paper Reflections Line
2300 S. Old Missouri Road
Springdale, AR 72764
www.dmdind.com
Paper Reflections Collage Papers™, cardstock, and ribbon

Dover Publications
31 East 2nd Street
Mineola, NY 11501-3852
www.doverpublications.com
Clip art books and CD-ROMs of copyright-free illustrations

Environmental Technology, Inc. (ETI)
South Bay Depot Road
Fields Landing, CA 95537-0365
707-443-9323
www.eti-usa.com
Envirotex Lite® epoxy resin, EasyCast Clear Casting Epoxy, molds, and pigments

Fire Mountain Gems™
One Fire Mountain Way
Grants Pass, OR 97526-2373
800-355-2137
www.firemountaingems.com
Beads, findings, stringing supplies, and books

Halstead Bead Inc. (HBI)
P.O. Box 2491
Prescott, AZ 86302
800-528-0535
www.halsteadbead.com
Metal beads, findings, and wire

Industrial Plastic Supply Co.
309 Canal Street
New York, NY 10013
212-226-2010
www.yourplasticsupermarket.com
Clear plastic cabochons

Jacquard Products/Rupert, Gibbon & Spider, Inc.
P.O. Box 425
Healdsburg, CA 95448
800-442-0455
www.jacquardproducts.com
Lumiere® and Neopaque® paints

Jones Tones
719-948-0048
www.jonestones.com
Clear acrylic cabochons and general art and craft supplies

Kemper Tools
13595 12th Street
Chino, CA 91710
909-627-6191
www.kempertools.com
Klay Kutters and other sculpting tools and supplies

Lazertran
650 8th Avenue
New Hyde Park, NY 11040
800-245-7547
www.lazertran.com
Waterslide decal paper: Silk, Regular, and Inkjet

The Leather Factory
800-433-3201
www.tandyleather.com
Leather, leatherworking tools, findings, and leather cord

Magenta Style
2275 Bombardier
Sainte-Julie, Quebec J3E 2J9
CANADA
450-922-5253
www.magentarubberstamps.com
Rubber stamps

Metalliferous, Inc.
34 West 46th Street
New York, NY 10036
888-944-0909
www.metalliferous.com
Jewelry findings, wire, tools, and supplies

National Artcraft Co.
7996 Darrow Road
Twinsburg, OH 44087
888-937-2723
www.nationalartcraft.com
Art and craft supplies, metallic rub-ons, and decorator chalks

Nature's Pressed
P.O. Box 212
Orem, UT 84059
800-850-2499
www.naturespressed.com
Pressed flowers and leaves

Plaid Enterprises, Inc.
3225 Westech Drive
Norcross, GA 30092
800-842-4197
www.plaidonline.com
Mod Podge® decoupage glue

Polyform Products Co.
1901 Estes
Elk Grove Village, IL 60007
www.sculpey.com
Sculpey™ and Premo™ clay products

Polymer Clay Express
13017 Wisteria Drive, Box 275
Germantown, MD 20874
800-844-0138
www.polymerclayexpress.com
Polymer clay, Clay Shapers, clay cutters, findings, and tools

Prairie Craft Company
P.O. Box 209
Florissant, CO 80816
800-779-0615
www.prairiecraft.com
Kato Polyclay™, Kato NuBlade™, tools, pattern cutters, and Dockyard carving tools

Ranger Industries, Inc.
15 Park Road
Tinton Falls, NJ 07724
800-244-2211
www.rangerink.com
Rubber stamping supplies and Suze Weinberg's embellishments

Rio Grande Industries, Inc.
7500 Bluewater Road
Albuquerque, NM 87121
800-545-6566
www.riogrande.com
Jewelry findings, gemstones, and general supplies

Scratch-Art® Co. Inc.
P.O. Box 303
Avon, MA 02322
508-583-8085
www.scratchart.com
Shade-Tex® Rubbing Plates

Shrinky Dinks®
K & B Innovations, Inc.
P.O. Box 223
North Lake, WI 53064-0223
www.shrinkydinks.com
262-966-0305
Shrinkable plastic

Soft Flex Company
P.O. Box 80
Sonoma, CA 95476
707-938-3539
www.softflexcompany.com
Soft Flex® Wire

Thunderbird Supply Co.
2311 Vassar NE
Albuquerque, NM 87107
800-545-7968
www.thunderbirdsupply.com
Jewelry findings, beads, and tools

Tsukineko®
17640 NE 65th Street
Redmond, WA 98052
800-769-6633
www.tsukineko.com
Rubber stamping supplies and StazOn™ ink

index

Acrylic cement, 18
Adhesives, 18–19
All-purpose white glue, 19
Asian-style floral pendant, 81–85

Bails, 12
Bangle bracelets, candy-stripe, 72–75
Barrette, leather, 115
Bauble, clear, in bracelet, 116–118
Bauble pendant, 119
Bead board, 15
Beaded gemstone necklace, 43–45
Beading basics, 30
Beading cord, silk, 17
Beads, crimp, 13, 16
Bead tips, 13
Bezel, wire-wrapped, 26–28
Bottle cap pins and pendants, 100–103
Bracelet(s)
  bangle, candy-stripe, 72–75
  Celtic knots, 61–64
  clear bauble, 116–118
  crystal flower, 29–33
  faux ivory, 57
  freshwater pearl, 23–25
  leather, 111–114
  leaves & violets, 34–37
  pressed flower, 107
  turquoise, 80
  vintage valentine, 120–122
Brand names, 18

Candy-stripe bangle bracelets, 72–75
Cast resin heart pendant, 97–99
Celtic earrings, 65
Celtic knots bracelet, 61–64
Celtic pendant, 65
Cement, acrylic, 18
Chain, 17
Chain-nose pliers, 14
Clasps, 13
Clay, polymer, 70–93
Clear bauble bracelet, 116–118
Cord,
  leather, 17
  silk beading, 17
Crimp beads, 13, 16
Crimping pliers, 14
Crocheted jewelry, 40–49
Crystal flower bracelet, 29–33

Decoupage glue, 19
Donut pendant, faux turquoise, 76–80

Earrings
  Celtic, 65
  Japanese woodcut, 86
  leaves & violets, 37–39
  pearl, 25
  pressed flower, 104–106
  valentine, 123
  vintage photo, 60
Ear wires, 12, 13
Epoxy resin, 18, 94
Eye pins, 12, 13

Fabric hem sealant, 19
Faux ivory bracelet, 57
Faux ivory scrimshaw pendant, 54–57
Faux turquoise donut pendant, 76–80
Findings, 12–13
Flat-nose pliers, 14
Floral pendant, Asian-style, 81–85
Flower ring, 33
Flowers, pressed, in pendant & earrings, 104–107
Freshwater pearl bracelet, 23–25

Gel-type adhesives, 18
Gem glue, 19
Getting started, 10–19
Glues, 18–19
Gold-stamped kanji pendant, 87–89

Head pins, 12, 13
Heart pendant, cast resin, 97–99
Hearts, shrink, 66–69
Hem sealant, 19

Japanese woodcut earrings, 86
Japanese woodcut pin, 85
Jewel glue, 19
Jewelry
  crocheted, 40–49
  polymer clay, 70–93
  resin, 94–107
  retro picture, 108–123
  shrink art, 50–69
  wire, 20–39
Jump rings, 12, 13

Kanji pendant, gold-stamped, 87–89

Laminate, 122
Leather, 112
Leather barrette, 115
Leather bracelet, 111–114
Leather cord, 17
Leather pendant, 115
Leaves & violets bracelet, 35–37
Leaves & violets earrings, 37–39

Mica pearl pendant, 90–93

Nail file, 15
Necklace(s)
  beaded gemstone, 43–45
  valentine, 123
  vintage photo, 60
Needle-nose pliers, 14
Needle tool, 15
Nylon-coated wire, 16, 17

Pearl bracelet, 23–25
Pearl earrings, 25
Pendant(s)
  bauble, 119
  bottle cap, 100–103
  Celtic, 65
  donut, faux turquoise, 76–80
  faux ivory scrimshaw, 54–57

floral, Asian-style, 81–85
  heart, cast resin, 97–99
  kanji, gold-stamped, 87–89
  leather, 115
  mica pearl, 90–93
  pressed flower, 104–106
  stone, 26–28
Pin(s)
  bottle cap, 100–103
  Japanese woodcut, 85
Pin backs, 12, 13
Pins,
  head, 12, 13
  eye, 12, 13
Pliers, 14
Polymer clay jewelry, 70–93
Pressed flower bracelet, 107
Pressed flower pendant & earrings, 104–106

Resin
  cast, heart pendant in, 97–99
  epoxy, 19, 96
Resin jewelry, 94–107
Retro picture jewelry, 108–123
Ring
  flower, 33
  '70s, 46–49
Rings
  jump, 12, 13
  split, 12
Round-nose pliers, 14
Ruler, 15

Scissors, 15
Scrimshaw pendant, faux ivory, 54–57
Sealant, fabric hem, 19
'70s ring, 46–49
Shrink art jewelry, 50–69
Shrink hearts, 66–69
Silk beading cord, 17
Split rings, 12
Stone pendant, 26–28
Stringing materials, 16–17
Super glue, 18

That '70s ring, 46–49
Thread, 17
Tools, 14–15
Turquoise, faux, donut pendant in, 76–80
Turquoise bracelet, 80
Tweezers, 15

Valentine earrings, 123
Valentine necklace, 123
Vintage photo jewelry, 58–60
Vintage valentine bracelet, 120–122

White glue, all-purpose, 19
Wire, nylon-coated, 16, 17
Wire cutters, 14, 15
Wire jewelry, 20–39
Wires, ear, 12, 13
Wire-wrapped bezel, 26–28
Woodcut, Japanese, 85–86